LECTIONES MEMORABILES

Volume II

*Selections from Horace,
Lucretius, Seneca, Suetonius,
and Tacitus*

LECTIONES MEMORABILES

Lectiones Memorabiles, Volume I:
Selections from Catullus, Cicero, Livy, Ovid,
Propertius, Tibullus, and Vergil (2015)

Lectiones Memorabiles, Volume II:
Selections from Horace, Lucretius, Seneca,
Suetonius, and Tacitus (2015)

LECTIONES MEMORABILES

VOLUME II

*Selections from Horace,
Lucretius, Seneca, Suetonius,
and Tacitus*

Yasuko Taoka

Bolchazy-Carducci Publishers, Inc.
Mundelein, Illinois USA

Editor: Laurel Draper
Contributing Editor: Timothy Beck
Design & Layout: Adam Phillip Velez
Maps: Mapping Specialists
Cover Graphic: The City of Rome's coat of arms on the Vatican's Porta Angelica (Wikimedia Commons)

Lectiones Memorabiles, Volume II:
Selections from Horace, Lucretius, Seneca,
Suetonius, and Tacitus

Yasuko Taoka

© 2015 Bolchazy-Carducci Publishers, Inc.
All rights reserved.

This work has been developed independently from and is not endorsed by the International Baccalaureate (IB).

Bolchazy-Carducci Publishers, Inc.
1570 Baskin Road
Mundelein, Illinois 60060
www.bolchazy.com

Printed in the United States of America
2015
by United Graphics

ISBN 978-0-86516-830-5

Library of Congress Cataloging-in-Publication Data

Lectiones memorabiles.
　　volumes cm
　Contents: Volume 1. Selections from Catullus, Cicero, Livy, Ovid, Propertius, Tibullus, and Vergil / Marianthe Colakis.
　ISBN 978-0-86516-829-9 (v.1 : pbk. : alk. paper) 1. Latin language--Readers. 2. Latin literature. 3. Latin literature--History and criticism. I. Colakis, Marianthe.
　PA2095.L375 2015
　478.6'421--dc23

2015010471

Contents

List of Maps and Illustrations vii
Preface ix

— History —

Introduction to History. 3
Tacitus 5
   Introduction to Tacitus. 5
   Annales 2.70–73, 82–83; 3.1–6, 10–18
      (SL and HL). 6
Suetonius. 47
   Introduction to Suetonius 47
   Tiberius 22–26, 33–36, 39–42, 52–53
      (HL Only). 48

— Good Living —

Introduction to Good Living 73
Lucretius. 75
   Introduction to Lucretius 75
   De Rerum Natura 1.54–135; 2.1–61
      (SL and HL). 78
Horace 97
   Introduction to Horace. 97
   Carmina 1.9; 2.16; 3.26; 4.7 (SL and HL) 100
Seneca. 115
   Introduction to Seneca 115
   Epistulae Morales 1, 16 (SL and HL). 118
   Introduction to *De Tranquillitate Animi*. 131
   De Tranquillitate Animi 2–3 (HL Only). 132

Appendix 1: Historical Timeline 149
Appendix 2: Meter 153
Appendix 3: Glossary of Rhetorical Terms, Figures of Speech,
    and Metrical Devices 155
Appendix 4: Family Tree of the Julio-Claudians 157

List of Maps and Illustrations

— Map —

The Mediterranean. xi

— Illustrations —

Head of Germanicus. 1
Alexander the Great 13
Tiberius. 17
Sestertius 65
Portrait of Epicurus 71
Athenian agora 77
The sacrifice of Iphigenia 85
House of Horace, Venosa 99
The Pantheon, Rome 103
Achilles statue, Corfu 109
Seneca. 117
Gladiators mosaic 143

Preface

Ancient Roman texts contain valuable insights into human psychology that are relevant even today. Historical works make striking observations about the personal motivations behind social and political actions; philosophical works acknowledge the influence and importance of our inner emotional workings while exhorting us to apply logical reasoning to attain distance from the damage our emotions may wreak on our happiness.

Both historical and philosophical writing is represented in this volume, which seeks to aid students preparing for the International Baccalaureate examinations in "History" and "Good Living." This volume is also appropriate for advanced high school students or intermediate-level college students seeking to read a variety of Roman works. The authors represented herein include Tacitus, Suetonius, Lucretius, Horace, and Seneca. Introductions to each section discuss facets of the genres of historical and philosophical writing; author introductions provide biographical and stylistic information on the author; introductions to each passage situate the selections within the larger scope of Roman literature, philosophy, and history.

Supplementary features serve to provide readers with additional information: a Glossary of Rhetorical Terms and Figures of Speech, which defines the terms in small capital letters in the commentary; a Metrical Appendix, which explains all meters used in the poetry selections; a timeline that provides an overview of significant events and people relevant to this volume; and a family tree that explicates the relationships of members of the Julio-Claudian family. Citations in the commentary to Allen and Greenough give grammatical guidance for difficult or unusual constructions. James B. Allen and J. H. Greenough's *New Latin Grammar* (1888, 1916), now in the public domain, is readily accessible online and is available in print from several publishers. It is often recommended to intermediate and advanced students of Latin as a grammar reference.

In closing, the contributions of those whose names do not appear on this volume's cover ought to be noted. This project is the brainchild of Bolchazy-Carducci, and I thank them for entrusting me with it. I also thank Laurel Draper for her tireless work on its behalf. The entire B-C family has been most welcoming. My friends, colleagues, and students at Southern Illinois University have provided me with ample support. Writing a commentary on the internal psychology and motivations behind life choices necessitates inflicting such conversations upon one's friends, and I thank mine for their generosity and patience.

— The Mediterranean —

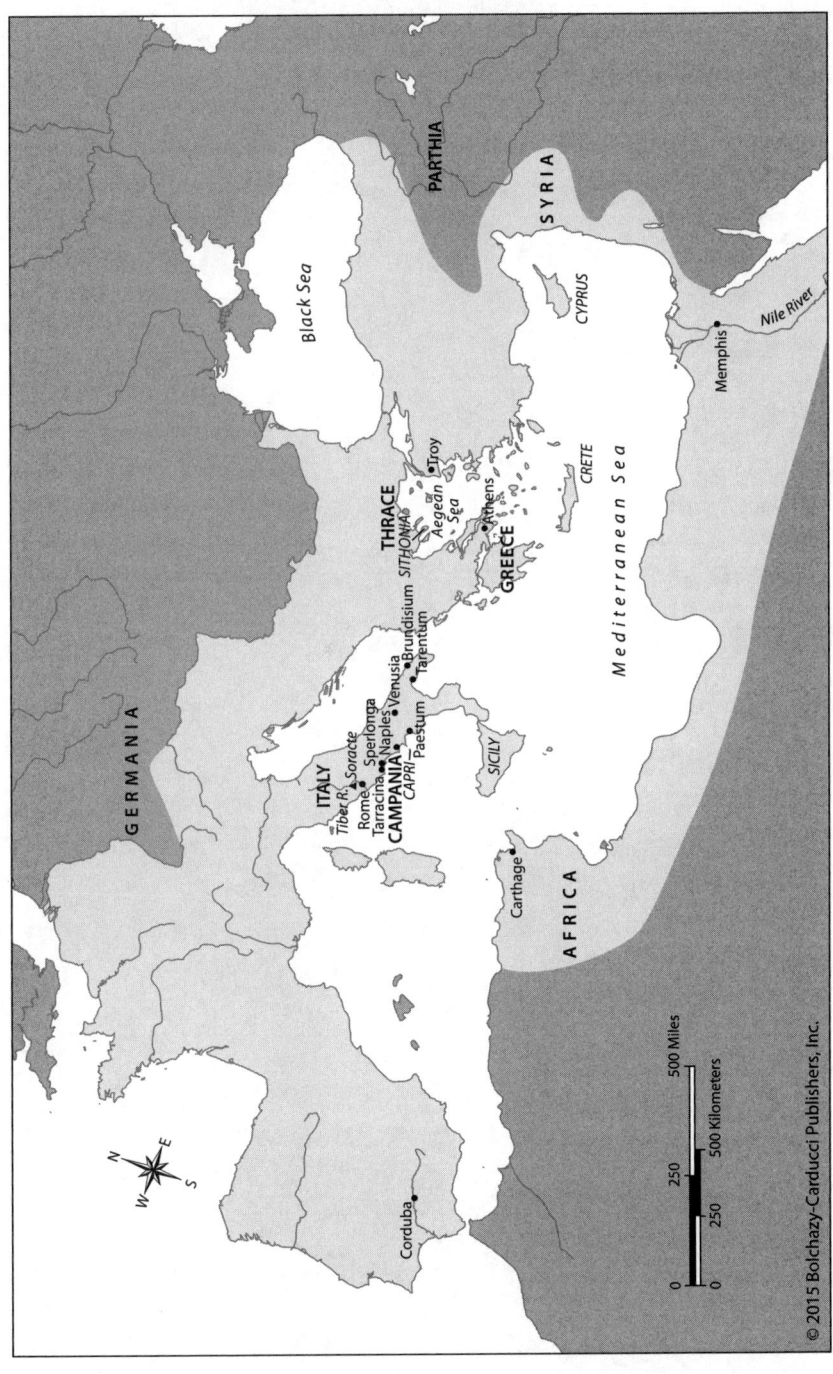

History

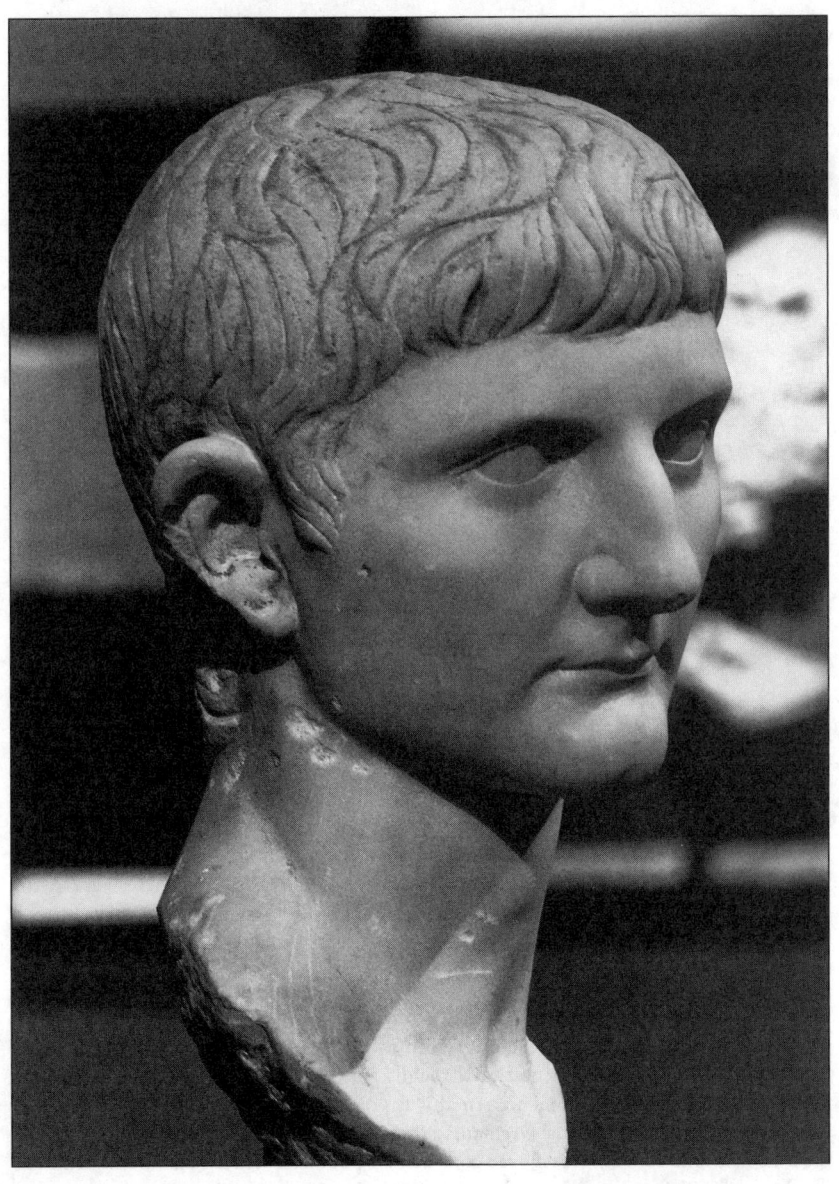

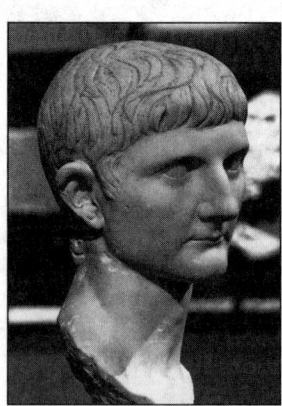

Head of Germanicus
ca. 14–ca. 23 CE.
(Wikimedia Commons)

Germanicus Julius Caesar, born Nero Claudius Drusus (ca. 15 BCE–19 CE), became a member of the Julian line of succession through adoption. He inherited his name from his father, who received the agnomen Germanicus posthumously in 9 BCE in recognition of military successes in Germania. Germanicus held several military and civic offices, including proconsul and consul, and enjoyed considerable popularity among Rome's citizens. His death, as we will see, was a cause of great public mourning by the Romans.

Introduction to History

The telling of history in the ancient world (termed "historiography") is significantly different from our modern conceptions of history. If you read a history textbook today, its tone and treatment of the material will not sound much like what we find in the selections from Tacitus and Suetonius below. While modern history texts are descended from Tacitus's annalistic history (for example, history books that proceed chronologically through time) or Suetonius's biographies (our modern biographies), there is much that is different. Consider, for example, the treatment of facts, sources, and speeches. We in the modern world are fixated on the precise reporting of facts and figures, but in the ancient world these numbers were less accurate. Likewise, in the modern world, the attribution of information to specific and credible sources is of utmost importance; on the other hand, ancient historians often report that "some people" were the source of information. Finally, while the lack of a flawless transcript for speeches in ancient historiography is not surprising given the lack of recording equipment, we find that ancient historians are often even more liberal in their understanding of accuracy in speeches: They preferred to transmit the general impression of what was—or should have been—said, rather than a verbatim transcript. While the lack of accuracy may seem shocking to us, these ancient historiographical traditions can be traced back to Greek historians like Herodotus and Thucydides. In ancient historiography, the general tone and characteristics were deemed more important for the transmission of truth than bare facts.

Do you agree with these ancient theories of historiography? Try it for yourself: Tell a story about something in the past. First, tell the story using only verifiable and objective facts. Then, tell it again, embellishing personalities and fudging facts in order to make your point. Which version do you like better? What are the strengths and weaknesses of each version? Keep these comparisons in mind as you consider the selections below.

Appendix 4 contains a family tree that shows the relationships of various members of the Julio-Claudian family. Readers are encouraged to refer to this appendix as needed for a reminder of the relationships of some of the individuals discussed in the History selections.

TACITUS

Annales 2.70–73, 82–83; 3.1–6, 10–18
Standard Level and Higher Level

— Introduction to Tacitus —

About the life of Gaius (or Publius; both are attested) Cornelius Tacitus we know very little. He was born, we believe, in the provinces, during Nero's reign; the majority of his adulthood was spent in Rome under the rule of the Flavians and his career as a historian bloomed in the time of Trajan. Tacitus launched his writing career toward the end of a career in politics. He began by writing the shorter monographs *Agricola* and *Germania*, then shifted gears for the stylistically very different *Dialogus de Oratoribus*. His crowning achievements are the *Historiae* and *Annales*, covering the Flavian and Julio-Claudian dynasties, respectively.

As our primary historical source for the Julio-Claudian era, Tacitus's account of its events and personalities has had a great impact on our understanding of the Julio-Claudians. His reading of Tiberius as a paranoid recluse, for example, has colored history's opinion of him. Tacitus tends to view history from a psychological or personal angle, and thus he finds that individual motivations are a driving force for history. In the selections below, pay particular attention to Tacitus's characterization of Tiberius, Germanicus, and Piso, and how their internal psychology influences their actions. The three intersect with each other chiefly through their jealousy and competitive feelings for one another. Tiberius, although he is emperor of Rome, is dogged by the desires of the populace for Tiberius's adoptive son Germanicus to be the emperor instead. When Piso disregards Germanicus's directives for the province of Syria, Germanicus is insulted. When Piso comes under suspicion for Germanicus's death, Tiberius seeks to distance himself from the disgraced official.

Tacitus's style of writing is famously idiosyncratic, as we will see. He has a tendency to vary his constructions, omit verbs, and use indirect speech.

— *Annales* 2.70–73 —

In this first selection, Tacitus continues to develop his characterization of Germanicus, who was first introduced in Book 1. The year is 19 CE, and the place is Syria. Tensions between Germanicus and Piso are coming to a head: As the new governor of Syria, Piso changed the provincial arrangements set up by Germanicus's consular **maius imperium** *over the East, which predictably angered Germanicus. Meanwhile, Piso, with the help of his wife, seems to have been machinating against Germanicus.*

[70] ea Germanico haud minus ira quam per metum accepta. si limen obsideretur, si effundendus spiritus sub oculis inimicorum foret, quid deinde miserrimae coniugi, quid infantibus liberis eventurum? lenta videri veneficia:
5   festinare et urgere, ut provinciam, ut legiones solus habeat. sed non usque eo defectum Germanicum, neque praemia caedis apud interfectorem mansura. componit epistulas quis amicitiam ei renuntiabat: addunt plerique iussum provincia decedere.

1   **ea:** refers to the allegations in the section immediately prior (2.69), namely that Piso wanted Germanicus dead, that he was actively working toward that end through the use of poison and witchcraft, and that he had sent spies to track Germanicus's condition.

   Germanico: an example of Tacitus's unusual style; we would expect **ab** with an ablative of agent and a passive verb.

   ira quam per metum: The avoidance of strict grammatical parallelism is very Tacitean. Moreover, what insights into Tacitus's characterization of Germanicus can we draw from this observation about his reaction to the rumors?

2   **accepta:** Understand **sunt**.

   si ... obsideretur: What does the mood of this verb (and **foret** in the next clause) tell us about the type of condition to which these protases belong? How does the mood of these verbs characterize

Germanicus's mindset? Moreover, how does the military META-
PHOR **limen obsideretur** contribute to the characterization of
Germanicus?

3 **inimicorum:** Piso's agents, but the word choice also contributes to
the military METAPHOR of **limen obsideretur**.

foret: with **effundendus**, forms a passive periphrastic construction; the choice of tense (**foret** rather than **esset**) makes clear that
these events would take place in the future (as with **eventurum**,
also in this sentence).

3-4 **coniugi ... liberis:** Germanicus's wife was Agrippina the Elder,
granddaughter of Augustus. They had six children who survived past
childhood, including the future emperor Caligula. Their daughter
Agrippina the Younger would give birth to the last of the Julio-
Claudian emperors, Nero. See Appendix 4: Family Tree of the
Julio-Claudians (page 157).

4-5 **videri ... festinare ... urgere:** indirect statement, continuing Germanicus's thoughts from the previous sentence. **Veneficia** is the subject accusative of **videri**; the subject of the latter two infinitives, and
of **habeat**, is Piso. The next sentence is also in indirect statement,
hence **Germanicum** is the subject accusative and **defectum** [**esse**]
is the infinitive.

6 **eo:** commonly with **usque**: "to that end," "to such a point." It refers
back to the result clause in the previous sentence, namely, to the
point that he would leave Piso to his own devices in Syria.

6-7 **praemia ... mansura:** As with **ira** above, Germanicus's resolve not
to let Piso profit from his crime characterizes Germanicus as virtu-
ous and brave.

8 **quis:** an alternative form for **quibus**.

addunt: introduces an indirect statement, for which **iussum** [**esse**]
is the infinitive verb and an understood **Pisonem** is the subject
accusative.

10 nec Piso moratus ultra navis solvit moderabaturque cursui quo propius regrederetur, si mors Germanici Syriam aperuisset.

[71] Caesar paulisper ad spem erectus, dein fesso corpore, ubi finis aderat, adsistentis amicos in hunc modum
15 adloquitur: "si fato concederem, iustus mihi dolor etiam adversus deos esset, quod me parentibus, liberis, patriae intra iuventam praematuro exitu raperent: nunc scelere Pisonis et Plancinae interceptus ultimas preces pectoribus vestris relinquo: referatis patri ac fratri, quibus acerbitatibus
20 dilaceratus, quibus insidiis circumventus miserrimam vitam pessima morte finierim. si quos spes meae, si quos propinquus sanguis, etiam quos invidia erga viventem movebat, inlacrimabunt quondam florentem et tot bellorum superstitem muliebri fraude cecidisse. erit vobis locus
25 querendi apud senatum, invocandi leges.

10   **navis:** accusative plural.

   cursui: Moderabatur takes the dative.

11   **regrederetur:** imperfect subjunctive in a relative clause of purpose (A&G §531.2.a). Here (as Germanicus's internal monologue above) is an example of Tacitus's interest in the psychology behind historical events and figures: Piso takes his time leaving Syria so that, should Germanicus die (and Germanicus's order thus become nullified), the return trip to Syria would be shorter.

11–12   **regrederetur ... aperuisset:** The tenses of these subjunctive verbs are governed by indirect statement—these are Piso's thoughts. For the tenses and moods of verbs in conditions in indirect discourse, see A&G §589.2.a.3.

13   **Caesar:** refers to Germanicus, who had been renamed Germanicus Julius Caesar upon his adoption by Tiberius.

ad spem: an important word for Germanicus, who is identified throughout the first two books of the *Annales* as the PERSONIFICATION of hope: hope for a different emperor than the peculiar and isolated Tiberius; hope for renewing the lost Republic.

14 **adsistentis:** accusative plural, modifying **amicos**.

15 **fato:** in contrast to **scelere** in the parallel clause (line 17); thus **fato** refers to a natural death, in the natural course of events. The subjunctive mood of **concederem**, however, indicates that Germanicus does not believe that his death is natural.

mihi: dative of possession.

16 **quod:** introduces a substantive clause expressing Germanicus's imaginary complaint against the gods, who are the subject of **raperent**.

17 **nunc:** not so much temporal as rhetorical: "but as it is"; it places emphasis on the second word of the clause, **scelere**. Notice the departure from Tacitean style in this speech: Germanicus's dying declaration is full of parallel structures and balanced clauses. Why would Tacitus use this different, older (some might say "Ciceronian") prose style for Germanicus?

18 **Plancinae:** Piso's wife, who allegedly exercised witchcraft against Germanicus.

19 **patri ac fratri:** his adoptive father Tiberius and adoptive brother Drusus the Younger.

quibus: indirect questions, as indicated by the mood of **finierim**.

20–21 **miserrimam ... pessima:** Notice the two superlatives in close proximity.

21 **si quos:** This condition has three protases, arranged in a Ciceronian TRICOLON CRESCENDO. The TRICOLON employs ANAPHORA (**si quos**), with slight VARIATIO in the final colon (**etiam quos**), further emphasizing it. **quos** = **aliquos**; recall the mnemonic rhyme "after **si, nisi, num,** and **ne, ali-** takes a holiday" (or "all the **ali**s fall away").

22 **viventem:** Understand **me**.

24 **muliebri fraude:** Plancina's witchcraft.

25 **querendi ... invocandi:** Notice, again, the balanced parallelism so prevalent throughout this speech.

non hoc praecipuum amicorum munus est, prosequi
defunctum ignavo questu, sed quae voluerit meminisse,
quae mandaverit exequi. flebunt Germanicum etiam ignoti:
vindicabitis vos, si mepotius quam fortunam meam fovebatis.
30 ostendite populo Romano divi Augusti neptem eandemque
coniugem meam, numerate sex liberos. misericordia cum
accusantibus erit fingentibusque scelesta mandata aut non
credent homines aut non ignoscent." iuravere amici dextram
morientis contingentes spiritum ante quam ultionem
35 amissuros.

[72] tum ad uxorem versus per memoriam sui, per communis
liberos oravit exueret ferociam, saevienti fortunae
summitteret animum, neu regressa in urbem aemulatione
potentiae validiores inritaret. haec palam et alia secreto per
40 quae ostendisse credebatur metum ex Tiberio. neque multo
post extinguitur, ingenti luctu provinciae et circumiacentium
populorum. indoluere exterae nationes regesque: tanta illi
comitas in socios, mansuetudo in hostis: visuque et auditu
iuxta venerabilis, cum magnitudinem et gravitatem summae
45 fortunae retineret, invidiam et adrogantiam effugerat.

[73] funus sine imaginibus et pompa per laudes ac memoriam
virtutum eius celebre fuit. et erant qui formam, aetatem,
genus mortis, ob propinquitatem etiam locorum in quibus
interiit, magni Alexandri fatis adaequarent. nam utrumque
50 corpore decoro, genere insigni, haud multum triginta annos
egressum, suorum insidiis externas inter gentis occidisse:

26 **munus:** here, specifically a tribute to the dead.

prosequi: The entire infinitive clause defines **hoc** from the previous clause. **Prosequi** is contrasted with two more infinitives (**meminisse, exequi**) that define the duties of the living to the dead. **Exequi** echoes **prosequi** as a compound of **sequor**.

30 **divi Augusti neptem:** Germanicus's wife, Agrippina the Elder, was Augustus's granddaughter: Her parents were Marcus Agrippa and Julia, Augustus's daughter by Scribonia.

33 **iuravere:** syncopated form of **iuraverunt**; introduces an indirect statement, for which **amissuros** [**esse**] is the infinitive verb and an understood **se** is the subject accusative.

37 **exueret:** imperfect subjunctive in indirect command governed by **oravit**; the subject is Agrippina.

39 **haec palam:** The dying Germanicus modulates his words to Agrippina; he recommends that she yield to fate and not challenge those more powerful in Rome. In private, however, he suspects that Tiberius may be responsible for his death.

42 **indoluere:** syncopated form of **indoluerunt**. This sentence serves as an initial eulogy for Germanicus. Tacitus catalogs Germanicus's near-improbable virtues: that he was beloved both among allies and enemies; that he achieved the greatest accomplishments without inciting envy.

46 **funus:** Germanicus's funeral mirrors his life with its emphasis on character and substance over the trappings of fame and fortune.

47 **erant:** When **sum** is used existentially ("there is/are"), as here, it tends to come earlier in the sentence. The subject is an understood **ei**, antecedent of a relative clause of characteristic introduced by **qui**.

49 **magni Alexandri:** As Tacitus will shortly explain in greater detail, Alexander the Great (Alexander III of Macedon) also died young, purportedly of poisoning, on travels to the East. More to the point, the implication is not only that the two died similarly (**fatis**), but that they also lived similarly.

utrumque: accusative subject of extended indirect discourse, reporting the words of those who compared Germanicus to Alexander.

sed hunc mitem erga amicos, modicum voluptatum, uno
matrimonio, certis liberis egisse, neque minus proeliatorem,
etiam si temeritas afuerit praepeditusque sit perculsas tot
55 victoriis Germanias servitio premere. quod si solus
arbiter rerum, si iure et nomine regio fuisset, tanto
promptius adsecuturum gloriam militiae quantum clementia,
temperantia, ceteris bonis artibus praestitisset. corpus
antequam cremaretur nudatum in foro Antiochensium,
60 qui locus sepulturae destinabatur, praetuleritne veneficii
signa parum constitit; nam ut quis misericordia in
Germanicum et praesumpta suspicione aut favore in Pisonem
pronior, diversi interpretabantur.

52 **hunc:** refers to Germanicus, who is compared favorably to Alexander: high praise indeed. The first half of this sentence praises his civic conduct, while the latter relates his military prowess.

54 **praepeditus sit:** governs the infinitive **premere** (line 55).

55 **quod:** "but."

56 **regio:** not the noun, but the adjective **regius**.

tanto: ablative of degree of difference with the comparative adverb **promptius**; it also anticipates its correlative **quantum**.

57 **adsecuturum:** Understand **fuisse**; indirect discourse continues, and Germanicus is still the subject. Recall that the accusative-infinitive construction is not used in dependent clauses (e.g., **si**-clauses) in indirect discourse.

60 **praetuleritne:** perfect subjunctive in indirect question, governed by **parum constitit**.

63 **diversi interpretabantur:** Tacitus astutely observes that an individual's inclination toward Germanicus or Piso influenced his interpretation of the physical evidence upon Germanicus's body.

Alexander the Great (Wikimedia Commons)

Alexander the Great's remarkable success as a military commander and as the founder of a vast empire caused many Romans to admire him. This sculpture, by Sir John Robert Steell (1804–1891), depicts Alexander with his beloved horse Bucephalas. Following Bucephalas's death, Alexander founded the city of Bucephala in what is now Pakistan or India; its exact location is unknown.

— *Annales* 2.82–83 —

In response to news of Germanicus's death, there is an outpouring of grief from the Roman populace. As the son of a successful general and himself a general, Germanicus was particularly popular among the military and the general citizenry, and they now appear in droves to mourn his death. Tacitus's own view of this mourning may be read as somewhat skeptical: He seems almost to view it as excessive.

[82] at Romae, postquam Germanici valetudo percrebuit cunctaque ut ex longinquo aucta in deterius adferebantur, dolor, ira, et erumpebant questus. ideo nimirum in extremas terras relegatum, ideo Pisoni permissam
5 provinciam; hoc egisse secretos Augustae cum Plancina sermones. vera prorsus de Druso seniores locutos: displicere regnantibus civilia filiorum ingenia, neque ob aliud interceptos quam quia populum Romanum aequo iure complecti reddita libertate agitaverint.

2 **ex longinquo ... deterius:** another astute psychological observation from Tacitus.

4 **relegatum:** Understand **fuisse**; the infinitive verb in indirect statement elaborates the content of the **questus**. When news of Germanicus's death breaks out at Rome, rumors—as they still do today in the wake of breaking news—fly rampant, not only blaming Piso and Plancina, but also implicating the imperial family. Notice that Tacitus, while including these accusations in his text, insulates himself from them by reporting them in indirect statement.

6 **vera:** Imagine scare quotes around this word. This statement, too, is in indirect statement: Tacitus does not claim that these accusations are true, merely that the speakers believe them to be so. The contents of **vera**, elaborated in the next clauses, are doubly distanced from Tacitus: "People gossiped that the elders had been right, when they said that..."

Druso: Germanicus's father, Nero Claudius Drusus. He was in the midst of a campaign that restored Roman honor in Germania (for which he earned the posthumous cognomen "Germanicus," which his son inherited) when he died suddenly. His death, too, was alleged to have been orchestrated by a member of the imperial family, this time Augustus, whom he had recently criticized. Thus **regnantibus** refers to Augustus and Tiberius (who is, ironically, Drusus's brother), and **filiorum** to their adoptive sons, Drusus and Germanicus, respectively.

7 **civilia ... ingenia:** "democratic tendencies"; Tacitus previously employs the term for both Drusus and Germanicus at *Annales* 1.33, when Germanicus is first introduced. Tacitus returns to the theme here at Germanicus's death: Both father and son represented for the Roman people the hope of a restoration of the Republic. This characteristic, of course, also made them unpalatable to the imperial family (**displicere regnantibus**).

neque ob aliud: anticipates **quam**.

9 **complecti ... agitaverint:** subject is understood **filii**, i.e., Drusus and Germanicus; the mood of **agitaverint** is determined by its usage in a dependent clause in indirect statement.

10 hos vulgi sermones audita mors adeo incendit ut ante
edictum magistratuum, ante senatus consultum sumpto
iustitio desererentur fora, clauderentur domus. passim
silentia et gemitus, nihil compositum in ostentationem;
et, quamquam neque insignibus lugentium abstinerent,
15 altius animis maerebant. forte negotiatores vivente adhuc
Germanico Syria egressi laetiora de valetudine eius attulere.
statim credita, statim vulgata sunt: ut quisque obvius,
quamvis leviter audita in alios atque illi in plures cumulata
gaudio transferunt. cursant per urbem, moliuntur
20 templorum foris; iuvat credulitatem nox et promptior inter
tenebras adfirmatio. nec obstitit falsis Tiberius donec
tempore ac spatio vanescerent: et populus quasi rursum
ereptum acrius doluit.

16 **attulere:** syncopated form of **attulerunt**.

17 **statim credita, statim vulgata sunt:** Tacitus makes here not only the specific point that the inhabitants of Rome were so enamored of Germanicus that they were willing to believe the impossible, but also the broader point about the insidiousness and potency of gossip. Notice that ANAPHORA and ASYNDETON emphasize the speed with which the rumor spread.

18 **leviter:** "unfounded," "unsubstantiated."

19 **cursant:** The subject is those who believe the gossip, but in effect it could also be the gossip itself.

20 **iuvat credulitatem nox:** an astute observation; how often have you found that you believe things at night that you would not in the light of day?

21 **falsis: Obstitit** takes the dative. Tiberius's inaction brings him in for tacit disapproval as the people are subjected to a second bereavement.

Tiberius (Wikimedia Commons)

This first-century CE portrait of the emperor Tiberius is housed in the Louvre Museum. It was discovered on Capri, an island in the Tyrrhenian Sea near Naples. Both Tiberius and his predecessor Augustus built villas on Capri. From 27 CE to his death in 37, Tiberius chose to live on the island rather than in Rome. Suetonius describes his reasons for doing so in *Tiberius* 40 (page 74).

[83] honores ut quis amore in Germanicum aut ingenio
25 validus reperti decretique: ut nomen eius Saliari carmine
caneretur; sedes curules sacerdotum Augustalium locis
superque eas querceae coronae statuerentur; ludos circensis
eburna effigies praeiret neve quis flamen aut augur in locum
Germanici nisi gentis Iuliae crearetur. arcus additi Romae et
30 apud ripam Rheni et in monte Syriae Amano cum
inscriptione rerum gestarum ac mortem ob rem publicam
obisse. sepulchrum Antiochiae ubi crematus, tribunal
Epidaphnae quo in loco vitam finierat. statuarum
locorumve in quis coleretur haud facile quis numerum
35 inierit. cum censeretur clipeus auro et magnitudine insignis
inter auctores eloquentiae, adseveravit Tiberius solitum
paremque ceteris dicaturum: neque enim eloquentiam
fortuna discerni et satis inlustre si veteres inter scriptores
haberetur. equester ordo cuneum Germanici appellavit
40 qui iuniorum dicebatur, instituitque uti turmae idibus Iuliis
imaginem eius sequerentur. pleraque manent: quaedam
statim omissa sunt aut vetustas oblitteravit.

24 **amore ... aut ingenio:** Tacitus's explanation of the extravagant number and variety of honors afforded Germanicus is both earnest and cynical: that some did it out of love for Germanicus, while others sought to demonstrate their cleverness with this exercise.

25–26 **ut ... caneretur:** a series of dependent noun clauses listing the **honores**.

25 **Saliari carmine:** The **carmen Saliare** was performed by the **Salii**, the priests of Mars, in their semiannual religious ritual, one of the oldest in Rome. This first sentence lists Germanicus's religious honors.

26	**sacerdotum Augustalium:** a new group of priests instituted by Tiberius.
27	**ludos circensis:** in particular, the parade that preceded the games.
29	**arcus:** Germanicus's architectural honors; the locations of the arches are significant as regions in which Germanicus excelled: Rome, Germania, Syria.
32–33	**ubi ... quo in loco:** another example of Tacitus's avoidance of strict parallelism.
34	**in quis:** syncopated form of **quibus**; the second **quis** in this sentence, however, is masculine nominative singular.
35	**clipeus:** not a working shield, but one upon which the portraits of illustrious men were depicted.
36	**solitum:** "customary," "usual."
38	**discerni:** passive infinitive in indirect statement; this entire latter half of the sentence reports Tiberius's reasoning for limiting the extravagance of Germanicus's **clipeus**. Once again Tiberius's reticence makes him appear stingy or jealous.
39	**cuneum:** an area of seats in a theater; the antecedent of **qui**.
40–41	**uti ... sequerentur:** This dependent noun clause reports the contents of the *equites*' order.
41	**manent:** Tacitus shifts to his present time to relate the contemporary status of the new practices.

— *Annales* 3.1–6 —

At long last, Germanicus's ashes are brought home to Rome by Agrippina, and they are greeted by throngs of mourners. Tacitus now treats Tiberius's response to Germanicus's death and uses it as an opportunity to analyze Tiberius's personality.

[1] nihil intermissa navigatione hiberni maris Agrippina
Corcyram insulam advehitur, litora Calabriae contra sitam.
illic paucos dies componendo animo insumit, violenta luctu
et nescia tolerandi. interim, adventu eius audito, intimus
quisque amicorum et plerique militares, ut quique sub
Germanico stipendia fecerant, multique etiam ignoti vicinis
e municipiis, pars officium in principem rati, plures
illos secuti, ruere ad oppidum Brundisium, quod naviganti
celerrimum fidissimumque adpulsu erat. atque ubi primum
ex alto visa classis, complentur non modo portus et proxima
mari, sed moenia ac tecta, quaque longissime prospectari
poterat, maerentium turba et rogitantium inter se silentione
an voce aliqua egredientem exciperent. neque satis constabat
quid pro tempore foret, cum classis paulatim successit, non
alacri, ut adsolet, remigio, sed cunctis ad tristitiam
compositis. postquam duobus cum liberis, feralem urnam
tenens, egressa navi defixit oculos, idem omnium gemitus;
neque discerneres proximos alienos, virorum feminarumve
planctus, nisi quod comitatum Agrippinae longo maerore
fessum obvii et recentes in dolore anteibant.

1   **nihil:** adverbial, "not at all"; Agrippina is returning to Rome with Germanicus's ashes and her children.

2   **Corcyram:** modern Corfu, an island off of the western coast of Greece, and east of the bootheel of Italy (ancient **Calabria**).

3–4	**violenta ... tolerandi:** a touching image of Agrippina, who needs a few days to compose herself as she tries to come to terms with her grief.
4	**intimus:** The list of the throng of mourners begins with only the closest friends, but by list's end expands to strangers who attend because it is "the thing to do." Tacitus's description of the final group expresses cynicism about groupthink.
7	**Principem** refers to Tiberius.
8	**ruere: ruerunt.**
	Brundisium: a port city on the east coast of Italy; a common point of departure and arrival to and from points east.
10–12	**portus ... poterat:** The magnitude of the number of locations flooded with mourners matches the earlier list of mourners.
12	**turba:** ablative, with **complentur**.
13	**Egredientem** refers to Agrippina, as she disembarks the ship.
	exciperent: imperfect subjunctive in an indirect question governed by **rogitantium** and introduced by **silentione an voce**.
14	**pro tempore:** "appropriate for the occasion."
16–17	**postquam ... oculos:** Tacitus's narrative in this sentence, building slowly until the final reveal of Agrippina, has a cinematic quality; we can imagine seeing first her children, then the urn, then finally her downcast eyes.
18	**discerneres:** imperfect subjunctive in the indefinite second person singular: "you could [not] distinguish between" (A&G §447.2). The direct objects (**proximos alienos**) are linked without **et**. Tacitus here surprises the reader after the earlier cynicism regarding the different groups of mourners gathered at Brundisium: Regardless of their closeness to Agrippina and Germanicus, all are moved alike to groan in unison for Agrippina's loss.
19	**nisi quod:** "except for the fact that."
20	**anteibant:** "surpassed."

[2] miserat duas praetorias cohortis Caesar, addito ut magistratus Calabriae Apulique et Campani suprema erga memoriam filii sui munia fungerentur. igitur tribunorum centurionumque umeris cineres portabantur; praecedebant incompta signa, versi fasces; atque ubi colonias transgrederentur, atrata plebes, trabeati equites pro opibus loci vestem odores aliaque funerum sollemnia cremabant. etiam quorum diversa oppida, tamen obvii et victimas atque aras dis Manibus statuentes lacrimis et conclamationibus dolorem testabantur. Drusus Tarracinam progressus est cum Claudio fratre liberisque Germanici, qui in urbe fuerant. consules M. Valerius et M. Aurelius (iam enim magistratum occeperant) et senatus ac magna pars populi viam complevere, disiecti et ut cuique libitum flentes; aberat quippe adulatio, gnaris omnibus laetam Tiberio Germanici mortem male dissimulari.

[3] Tiberius atque Augusta publico abstinuere, inferius maiestate sua rati si palam lamentarentur, an ne omnium oculis vultum eorum scrutantibus falsi intellegerentur. matrem Antoniam non apud auctores rerum, non diurna actorum scriptura, reperio ullo insigni officio functam, cum super Agrippinam et Drusum et Claudium ceteri quoque consanguinei nominatim perscripti sint, seu valetudine praepediebatur seu victus luctu animus magnitudinem mali perferre visu non toleravit. facilius crediderim Tiberio et Augustae qui domo non excedebant, cohibitam, ut par maeror et matris exemplo avia quoque et patruus attineri viderentur.

21	**addito:** ablative absolute, followed by a subjunctive noun clause: "with the addition that."
27	**odores:** not the smell itself, but the substance burned to produce the smell.
28	**tamen obvii:** They met the funeral party despite their distance.
30	**Drusus:** Germanicus's adoptive brother, Tiberius's son; **Claudio fratre** is the future emperor Claudius; **liberis:** only two were with Agrippina.
	Tarracina is located on the western coast of Italy just south of Rome.
33	**occeperant:** The year is now 20 CE.
35	**gnaris omnibus:** ablative absolute, with **gnaris** introducing an indirect statement.
36	**Tiberio:** Rather than an ablative of agent, Tacitus opts for a dative (A&G §375). Nonetheless he makes a strong contention, not only that Tiberius was pleased at the elimination of Germanicus, but also that this was patently evident to the populace.
37	**Augusta:** Livia, Tiberius's mother and Augustus's wife.
38	**maiestate sua:** ablative of comparison.
38–39	**ne . . . intellegerentur:** a fear clause following **rati**, with the fear implied; another Tacitean slight against Tiberius.
40	**matrem Antoniam:** Germanicus's mother Antonia the Younger, daughter of Mark Antony and Octavia; accusative subject of indirect statement governed by **reperio**, for which the infinitive verb is **functam [esse]**.
	auctores rerum: "historians."
40–41	**diurna actorum scriptura:** "public papers of the state."
44	**praepediebatur:** The subject is Antonia.
46	**crediderim:** Note the mood of this verb; how might you translate this independent usage, accounting for its tense?
	Tiberio et Augustae: not to be taken with **crediderim**, but dative of agent with **cohibitam**.

[4] dies quo reliquiae tumulo Augusti inferebantur modo
per silentium vastus, modo ploratibus inquies; plena urbis
itinera, conlucentes per campum Martis faces. illic miles cum
armis, sine insignibus magistratus, populus per tribus
concidisse rem publicam, nihil spei reliquum clamitabant,
promptius apertiusque quam ut meminisse imperitantium
crederes. nihil tamen Tiberium magis penetravit quam studia
hominum accensa in Agrippinam, cum decus patriae, solum
Augusti sanguinem, unicum antiquitatis specimen
appellarent versique ad caelum ac deos integram illi subolem
ac superstitem iniquorum precarentur.

[5] fuere qui publici funeris pompam requirerent
compararentque quae in Drusum patrem Germanici honora
et magnifica Augustus fecisset. ipsum quippe asperrimo
hiemis Ticinum usque progressum neque abscedentem a
corpore simul urbem intravisse; circumfusas lecto
Claudiorum Lioviorumque imagines; defletum in foro,
laudatum pro rostris, cuncta a maioribus reperta aut quae
posteri invenerint cumulata: at Germanico ne solitos quidem
et cuicumque nobili debitos honores contigisse.

49 **tumulo Augusti:** the mausoleum of Augustus in the Campus Martius.

50 **per silentium ... ploratibus** is an example of Tacitean VARIATIO.

50–51 **plena urbis itinera:** reminiscent of the earlier flooding of Brundisium by the throngs of mourners.

53 **concidisse ... reliquum:** The indirect statement here encapsulates the ideals that Germanicus represented for the masses. Tacitus thus consistently depicts him as a foil for Tiberius.

54-55	**ut ... crederes:** dependent noun clause, the comparison after **quam**; Tacitus again reiterates the impetuousness of voicing these opinions before Tiberius and others in power.
54	**Meminisse**, as a verb of remembering, takes the genitive.
55	**nihil ... penetravit:** Tacitus again reiterates Tiberius's jealousy of Germanicus's (and Agrippina's) popularity.
56-58	**cum ... appellarent:** What is the import of the subjunctive mood of **appellarent** in this **cum**-clause? The word choice is very loaded: **patriae, Augusti, antiquitatis**. Notice also the insistence upon her singular exemplarity: **solum, unicum. Solum Augusti sanguinem** is not technically correct, but Tacitus may have meant to put such an exaggeration into the mouths of Agrippina's supporters, so great was their affection for her.
58-59	**integram ... iniquorum:** indirect statement governed by **precarentur**.
58	**Illi** refers to Agrippina.
59	**Superstitem** can take either the dative or, as here, the genitive.

Iniquorum is substantive here in the sense of "hostiles," "enemies." |
60	**fuere: fuerunt**, existential use of **sum**; **qui** introduces a relative clause of characteristic, common after existential **est**.
62-64	**ipsum ... progressum ... intravisse:** indirect statement, reporting the thoughts of the critics; the indirect statement continues through the end of this section. **Ipsum** is Tiberius, who rode out to meet Drusus's body; once again Tiberius's treatment of Germanicus seems to pale in comparison to Drusus's. **Quippe** nicely characterizes the mindset of the speakers, as do **ne ... quidem** and **sane** in the clauses that follow.
66-67	**reperta aut quae ... invenerint:** Rather than strict parallelism, Tacitus uses two different constructions: a participial clause and a relative clause; **cumulata** is the main verb for **cuncta**.
67	**at Germanico:** This begins a point-by-point comparison of the funerals of Drusus and Germanicus. The critics compare the splendor of the funerals, the distance traveled by imperial family members to accompany the body, and the public displays of sorrow.

sane corpus ob longinquitatem itinerum externis terris
70 quoquo modo crematum; sed tanto plura decora mox
tribui par fuisse quanto prima fors negavisset. non fratrem
nisi unius diei via, non patruum saltem porta tenus obvium.
ubi illa veterum instituta, propositam toro effigiem, meditata
ad memoriam virtutis carmina et laudationes et lacrimas vel
75 doloris imitamenta?

[6] gnarum id Tiberio fuit; utque premeret vulgi sermones,
monuit edicto multos inlustrium Romanorum ob rem
publicam obisse, neminem tam flagranti desiderio celebratum.
idque et sibi et cunctis egregium, si modus adiceretur. non
80 enim eadem decora principibus viris et imperatori populo quae
modicis domibus aut civitatibus. convenisse recenti dolori
luctum et ex maerore solacia; sed referendum iam animum ad
firmitudinem, ut quondam divus Iulius amissa unica filia, ut
divus Augustus ereptis nepotibus abstruserint tristitiam. nil
85 opus vetustioribus exemplis, quotiens populus Romanus cladis
exercituum, interitum ducum, funditus amissas nobilis familias
constanter tulerit. principes mortales, rem publicam aeternam
esse. proin repeterent sollemnia, et quia ludorum Megalesium
spectaculum suberat, etiam voluptates resumerent.

71 **par fuisse:** the main clause in the **tanto** clause; it introduces the indirect statement **decora ... tribui.**

fratrem: Drusus the Younger, Tiberius's biological son and Germanicus's adoptive brother; the contrast is with Tiberius himself, who traveled to northern Italy to meet Germanicus's father's body. **Patruum** is Tiberius, who is identified by his biological, rather than adoptive, relationship to Germanicus. **Tenus** takes the ablative and frequently follows its object.

73 **illa veterum instituta:** The list of five objects that follow enumerates the old traditions that were expected.

74–75 **vel doloris imitamenta:** another barely veiled critique of Tiberius (and Livia), who did not participate in the public mourning of Germanicus, and thereby appeared to feel no grief. This clause is put in the mouths of the critics, though it could just as easily have been Tacitus's opinion.

76 **id:** the complaints of the populace, particularly the last point, about his lack of public feeling; **utque** thus introduces a purpose clause.

77 **monuit edicto:** While Tiberius's advice is generally sound, i.e., that grief must come to an end and that life must go on, the manner of delivery (**edicto**) and the general rhetoric of his proclamation (e.g., **neminem tam flagranti desiderio celebratum**) depict him as a unidirectional ruler who shares little sympathy with the populace. This, of course, is in accordance with Tacitus's general characterization of Tiberius. The remainder of the section is in indirect statement, reporting Tiberius's proclamation.

79 **et sibi et cunctis:** datives of reference or of "the person judging" (A&G §378): "in his and in everyone's opinion."

80 **decora:** from **decorum**, not **decus:** "propriety"; Tiberius is here merely stating a fact obvious to him, but the sentiment comes off as classist in light of the republican hopes the people had for Germanicus, and the outpouring of grief from that sector.

81 **convenisse:** "was suited," "was fitting."

83 **ut:** "as"; **abstruserint** is subjunctive because of indirect discourse. Notice that Tiberius responds to the critiques of the populace point by point: He first disputes that Germanicus's funeral lacks the accustomed splendor; he then responds to those who find his mourning to be less expressive than Augustus's.

amissa unica filia: Julius Caesar's daughter Julia, who died in 54 BCE.

84 **divus Augustus ereptis nepotibus:** Lucius and Gaius Caesar, who died in 2 and 4 CE, respectively.

quotiens populus Romanus: Tiberius draws upon the Roman valorization of their self-restraint.

88 **repeterent:** imperfect subjunctive, reporting an original jussive subjunctive, **repetant**; **resumerent** is in the same construction.

— *Annales* 3.10–18 —

The narrative now turns to Germanicus's alleged poisoner Piso: There is an investigation into Germanicus's death, and Tiberius's stance on the allegations tells us much about his political maneuvering. Throughout these selections we can observe how Tacitus portrays Tiberius through his interactions with both Germanicus and Piso.

[10] postera die Fulcinius Trio Pisonem apud consules postulavit. contra Vitellius ac Veranius ceterique Germanicum comitati tendebant, nullas esse partis Trioni; neque se accusatores, sed rerum indices et testis mandata
5 Germanici perlaturos. ille dimissa eius causae delatione, ut priorem vitam accusaret obtinuit petitumque est a principe cognitionem exciperet. quod ne reus quidem abnuebat, studia populi et patrum metuens; contra Tiberium spernendis rumoribus validum et conscientiae matris
10 innexum esse; veraque aut in deterius credita iudice ab uno facilius discerni, odium et invidiam apud multos valere. haud fallebat Tiberium moles cognitionis quaque ipse fama distraheretur. igitur paucis familiarium adhibitis minas accusantium et hinc preces audit integramque causam
15 ad senatum remittit.

1   **Fulcinius Trio:** Tacitus first introduces him at *Annales* 2.28, as an eager and insidious informant.

2   **postulavit:** here, specifically, "to call to trial."

3   **nullas esse . . . :** indirect speech, reporting the rationale of Germanicus's friends; **Trioni** is dative of possession.

4–5   **mandata Germanici:** With his dying words, Germanicus accused Piso of poisoning him.

5   **dimissa . . . delatione:** ablative absolute.

6   **ut ... accusaret:** subjunctive noun clause, object of **obtinuit**.

7   **cognitionem exciperet:** Understand **ut** before the indirect command **cognitionem exciperet**; Tiberius, **princeps**, is the subject.

quod: a connective relative, equivalent to **et hoc** (A&G §308.f); it refers to the decision made in the previous sentence, that the investigation would be turned over to Tiberius.

8   **metuens:** Piso was likely right to be afraid of bias, based on the public outpouring of support for Germanicus and his survivors.

Tiberium: The remainder of the sentence is in indirect statement, reporting Piso's thought process.

9–10   **conscientiae matris innexum esse:** Piso/Tacitus saves the more damning thought for second: Not only is Tiberius free of bias against Piso, he is compromised in favor of Piso by Livia's implication.

10   **aut in deterius credita:** "from those assumed to be worse"; another Tacitean psychological observation, though here couched in Piso's thoughts. Do you agree with Tacitus's/Piso's assessment about the frivolity of the masses?

12–13   **quaque ipse fama distraheretur:** As above at 3.3 (page 22) and 3.6 (page 26), Tiberius is keenly aware of how he is regarded by the populace.

[11] atque interim Drusus rediens Illyrico, quamquam patres censuissent ob receptum Maroboduum et res priore aestate gestas ut ovans iniret, prolato honore urbem intravit.

post quae reo L. Arruntium, P. Vinicium, Asinium Gallum, Aeserninum Marcellum, Sex. Pompeium patronos petenti iisque diversa excusantibus M'. Lepidus et L. Piso et Livineius Regulus adfuere, arrecta omni civitate, quanta fides amicis Germanici, quae fiducia reo; satin cohiberet ac premeret sensus suos Tiberius. haud alias intentior populus plus sibi in principem occultae vocis aut suspicacis silentii permisit.

[12] die senatus Caesar orationem habuit meditato temperamento. patris sui legatum atque amicum Pisonem fuisse adiutoremque Germanico datum a se, auctore senatu, rebus apud Orientem administrandis. illic contumacia et certaminibus asperasset iuvenem exituque eius laetatus esset an scelere extinxisset, integris animis diiudicandum. "nam si legatus officii terminos, obsequium erga imperatorem exuit eiusdemque morte et luctu meo laetatus est, odero seponamque a domo mea et privatas inimicitias non vi principis ulciscar;

16   **Drusus:** In 3.7 Drusus had been dispatched to Illyricum (a province on the other side of the Adriatic Sea), whence he now returns. Piso had hoped, in 3.8, to meet Drusus before he could return to Rome, and to win him to his side.

17   **Maroboduum:** king of the Marcomanni, a Germanic tribe.

18   **ut ... iniret:** purpose clause.

19   **post quae:** another connective relative.

19–22 **Reo ... petenti** and **iis ... excusantibus** are ablative absolutes, as is **arrecta omni civitate.**

23   **satin:** Complementing Piso's skepticism about the populace, the populace worries about Tiberius's equanimity.

24   **haud alias:** adverbial, "never besides," "at no other time."

25   **occultae vocis aut suspicacis silentii:** partitive genitives with **plus** (A&G §346.a.2). An interesting apparent contradiction exists in that the two comparatives, **intentior** and **plus**, represent opposing actions: The people are more attentive to Tiberius, but they are more permissive of their own suspicions about him. They expect Tiberius to support Germanicus; what do you predict?

26   **senatus:** genitive.

   Caesar is here, as above, Tiberius.

27   **patris sui legatum:** Indirect speech begins here, lasting until the direct quotation begins in earnest at **nam si legatus . . .** The speech comprises the remainder of the section. The **patris** named here is Augustus. What do you think of this opening to the speech? What do you think Tiberius is attempting to accomplish with such an introduction? What is the modern equivalent of this kind of opening in, say, a murder case? (Note, however, that no charges have been filed—the senate is merely opening an investigation into Germanicus's death.)

30   **asperasset:** pluperfect subjunctive in an indirect question, governed by **diiudicandum**; there are two questions, the first a simple yes/no question ("whether"), the second a disjunction (**laetatus esset an . . . extinxisset**). Tiberius will push on this last disjunction—whether Piso was merely pleased at Germanicus's death or had caused it himself—for the remainder of the speech.

32–33   **si . . . exuit:** Tiberius uses the indicative mood for this condition (also **laetatus est**); he also uses the indicative for the other condition, **sin . . . detegitur**. Both are, in his presentation, live possibilities. This first condition, despite being the lesser of the two evils, certainly sounds reprehensible.

33   **odero: Odi** is a defective verb, having only a perfect system (A&G §205); thus **odero**, future perfect, is the equivalent of a future and parallel to **seponam** and **ulciscar**.

34–35   **privatas . . . principis:** Tiberius reiterates that Piso would still be punished, but he distinguishes between personal and official business.

sin facinus in cuiuscumque mortalium nece vindicandum detegitur, vos vero et liberos Germanici et nos parentes iustis solaciis adficite. simulque illud reputate, turbide et seditiose tractaverit exercitus Piso, quaesita sint per ambitionem studia militum, armis repetita provincia, an falsa haec in maius vulgaverint accusatores, quorum ego nimiis studiis iure suscenseo. nam quo pertinuit nudare corpus et contrectandum vulgi oculis permittere differrique etiam per externos tamquam veneno interceptus esset, si incerta adhuc ista et scrutanda sunt? defleo equidem filium meum semperque deflebo; sed neque reum prohibeo quo minus cuncta proferat, quibus innocentia eius sublevari aut, si qua fuit iniquitas Germanici, coargui possit, vosque oro ne, quia dolori meo causa conexa est, obiecta crimina pro adprobatis accipiatis. si quos propinquus sanguis aut fides sua patronos dedit, quantum quisque eloquentia et cura valet, iuvate periclitantem; ad eundem laborem, eandem constantiam accusatores hortor. id solum Germanico super leges praestiterimus, quod in curia potius quam in foro, apud senatum quam apud iudices de morte eius anquiritur; cetera pari modestia tractentur. nemo Drusi lacrimas, nemo maestitiam meam spectet, nec si qua in nos adversa finguntur."

36   **cuiuscumque mortalium:** Murder, Tiberius emphasizes, is to be avenged for any human, not only the beloved and famous such as Germanicus.

38   **adficite:** "furnish," "provide," with an ablative of instrument. Notice that Tiberius specifically underlines his relationship to Germanicus as a **parens**.

illud: points forward, to the indirect questions that follow; the three questions all concern the abuse of power for personal gain.

40   **an falsa haec:** Tiberius's motives and purpose are finally crystal clear.

40–41   **in maius:** "to a greater degree."

42   **suscenseo:** takes the dative. Tiberius moves now from merely accusing Germanicus's supporters of exaggeration to what he describes as "just anger" (**iure**) at their "zealotry" (**nimiis studiis**).

quo pertinuit: "what purpose did it have"; it takes the three infinitives **nudare, permittere,** and **differri,** the last of which introduces a conditional clause of comparison (A&G §524) introduced by **tamquam.** Tiberius uses a series of RHETORICAL QUESTIONS to criticize the motives behind Germanicus's funeral rites.

45   **defleo:** Tiberius returns to his love of Germanicus, whom he calls **filium meum.** What might be his motives behind this rhetoric?

46   **quo minus:** Verbs of prohibiting or refusing (e.g., **prohibeo**) frequently introduce clauses with **quin** or **quominus** and the subjunctive (A&G §558.b).

48–49   **quia dolori meo:** Is this a good reason to ask for what follows in the indirect command (**ne ... accipiatis**)?

49   **obiecta:** "charged," "alleged."

52   **ad eundem laborem, eandem constantiam:** While this sentiment seems to treat the two sides equally, it is clear by now that Tiberius has delivered a speech for the defense.

54   **quod:** introduces a substantive clause: "that."

56   **tractentur:** jussive subjunctive.

nemo ... nemo: Notice the frequent usage of ANAPHORA and parallelism as Tiberius's speech winds to a close: **in curia ... in foro, apud senatum ... apud iudices.**

57   **qua: aliqua** (after **si**), neuter plural subject of **finguntur.**

[13] exim biduum criminibus obiciendis statuitur utque sex dierum spatio interiecto reus per triduum defenderetur.
60 tum Fulcinius vetera et inania orditur, ambitiose avareque habitam Hispaniam; quod neque convictum noxae reo si recentia purgaret, neque defensum absolutioni erat si teneretur maioribus flagitiis. post quem Servaeus et Veranius et Vitellius consimili studio et multa eloquentia Vitellius
65 obiecere odio Germanici et rerum novarum studio Pisonem vulgus militum per licentiam et sociorum iniurias eo usque conrupisse ut parens legionum a deterrimis appellaretur; contra in optimum quemque, maxime in comites et amicos Germanici saevisse; postremo ipsum devotionibus et veneno
70 peremisse; sacra hinc et immolationes nefandas ipsius atque Plancinae, petitam armis rem publicam, utque reus agi posset, acie victum.

[14] defensio in ceteris trepidavit; nam neque ambitionem militarem neque provinciam pessimo cuique obnoxiam, ne
75 contumelias quidem adversum imperatorem infitiari poterat:

58–59   **sex ... interiecto:** ablative absolute.

Ut ... defenderetur is a noun clause, another subject (along with **biduum**) of **statuitur**. This section summarizes the case of the accusers.

60   **Fulcinius:** Trio, from section 10 above; recall that there he was placated by being allowed to present the case of Piso's prior offences.

60–61   **ambitiose ... Hispaniam:** indirect statement, reporting Piso's accusations. Fulcinius, to his credit, is attempting to build a pattern of behavior for Piso.

61   **noxae reo:** a double dative construction (A&G §382.1); similarly, **absolutioni** is a dative of purpose. Tacitus continues to stress the pointlessness of Fulcinius's contribution.

65   **obiecere:** syncopated form of **obiecerunt**; introduces the indirect statement that begins with **odio** and extends to the end of the section. These are their official charges against Piso.

        rerum novarum: political innovations, specifically, "revolution," considered potentially disruptive or problematic. **Sociorum** refers to those who lived in the provinces governed by Piso. These first two charges allege that by (1) allowing them to mistreat the provinces, he (2) corrupted his army.

68   **contra:** the third charge, that Piso was supremely cruel to the best officers, particularly those associated with Germanicus.

69   **postremo:** the final charge, that he had murdered Germanicus.

        devotionibus: "spells," "enchantments."

70   **sacra hinc:** describes the consequences of his crimes. Plancina is implicated here as the one who practices the witchcraft.

73   **defensio:** This section summarizes Piso's defense.

        ceteris: the rest of the charges (aside from the one refuted below).

solum veneni crimen visus est diluisse, quod ne accusatores
quidem satis firmabant, in convivio Germanici, cum super
eum Piso discumberet, infectos manibus eius cibos arguentes.
quippe absurdum videbatur inter aliena servitia et tot
80　adstantium visu, ipso Germanico coram, id ausum;
offerebatque familiam reus et ministros in tormenta
flagitabat. sed iudices per diversa implacabiles erant, Caesar
ob bellum provinciae inlatum, senatus numquam satis credito
sine fraude Germanicum interisse. . . . scripsissent
85　expostulantes, quod haud minus Tiberius quam Piso abnuere.
simul populi ante curiam voces audiebantur: non
temperaturos manibus si patrum sententias evasisset.
effigiesque Pisonis traxerant in Gemonias ac divellebant,
ni iussu principis protectae repositaeque forent. igitur inditus
90　lecticae et a tribuno praetoriae cohortis deductus est, vario
rumore custos saluti an mortis exactor sequeretur.

77–78　**in convivio ... cibos:** indirect statement, governed by **arguentes**. Tacitus admits that the case for poisoning seemed tenuous; notice touches that reveal skepticism, like **ne accusatores quidem** and **quippe absurdum videbatur**. Tacitus paints a rather implausible portrait of the crime scene.

80　**id ausum:** Recall that **audeo** is a semideponent verb: The perfect system is deponent, and thus is translated actively; the subject is thus Piso, and **id** is direct object.

81　**familiam:** his household, i.e., his slaves; **ministros** refers to the slaves who were attendants at the meal in question.

82　**per diversa:** The judges' (i.e., the senate's, including Tiberius) indecision is explained in the **ob** clause (for Tiberius) and the ablative absolute **credito** clause (for the rest of the senate).

84–85 **scripsissent expostulantes:** Before these words, a significant amount of text is missing. What seems to have transpired in the lacuna is that the senate demanded (**expostulantes**) to see the correspondence between Tiberius and Piso (**scripsissent**). Both Tiberius and Piso refuse. What are some reasons they might have refused to allow the senate to read their letters?

86–87 **non temperaturos ... evasisset:** indirect statement, reporting the **voces**. The subject of **evasisset** is Piso.

88 **Gemonias:** steps on the Aventine Hill, whither the bodies of executed criminals were taken to be thrown into the Tiber. The mob makes do with statues of Piso, since the real thing is contained within the Curia.

89 **ni:** "but that."

inditus: the subject of this sentence is Piso.

91 **sequeretur:** indirect question reporting the **vario rumore**; the subject is the praetorian escort.

[15] eadem Plancinae invidia, maior gratia; eoque ambiguum habebatur quantum Caesari in eam liceret. atque ipsa, donec mediae Pisoni spes, sociam se cuiuscumque fortunae
95 et si ita ferret comitem exitii promittebat; ut secretis Augustae precibus veniam obtinuit, paulatim segregari a marito, dividere defensionem coepit. quod reus postquam sibi exitiabile intellegit, an adhuc experiretur dubitans, hortantibus filiis durat mentem senatumque rursum
100 ingreditur; redintegratamque accusationem, infensas patrum voces, adversa et saeva cuncta perpessus, nullo magis exterritus est quam quod Tiberium sine miseratione, sine ira, obstinatum clausumque vidit, ne quo adfectu perrumperetur. relatus domum, tamquam defensionem in posterum
105 meditaretur, pauca conscribit obsignatque et liberto tradit; tum solita curando corpori exequitur. dein multam post noctem, egressa cubiculo uxore, operiri foris iussit; et coepta luce perfosso iugulo, iacente humi gladio, repertus est.

92 **gratia:** Plancina had a relationship with, and thus an ally in, Livia.
eoque: "and on that account," "and for that reason," "therefore."

93 **habebatur** is impersonal passive, introducing the indirect question **quantum ... liceret**.

In eam refers to the case against Plancina: "against her." The exploration into the psychological and interpersonal motivations behind political acts is a typical Tacitean form of analysis.

ipsa: Plancina.

94 **Spes** is nominative plural.

94–95 **Sociam ... exitii** is an indirect statement introduced by **promittebat**. Plancina plays the part of the ideal Roman wife, vowing to share the fate of her husband.

95   **ut:** "when"; fulfilling her role as the villainess of this story, Plancina is faithless even to her husband once her own safety is secured. Consider Tacitus's depiction of Plancina throughout these passages: How "accurate" do you think it is? What function does her character serve for the narrative?

98   **an adhuc experiretur dubitans:** As frequently in Tacitus, the verb governing indirect discourse (**dubitans**) comes after the indirect question (**an adhuc experiretur**).

101 **nullo:** ablative of instrument with **exterritus est**: "by nothing."

102 **Tiberium:** Notice how Tacitus contrasts the open aggression of Piso's adversaries and the senators with Tiberius's stony silence. Why might Piso be more frightened by Tiberius's demeanor than by the raging senators?

103 **quo: aliquo**, after **ne**, agreeing with **adfectu**; the **ne** clause expresses negative purpose.

104 **relatus:** subject is Piso.

Tamquam gives some hint of the events to come.

106–108 **dein ... repertus est:** Tacitus's reportage of Piso's final actions is simple and devoid of excessive ornamentation, lending clarity and determination to Piso's actions. Interestingly, the most crucial words, **perfosso iugulo**, are an ablative absolute.

[16] audire me memini ex senioribus visum saepius inter manus Pisonis libellum quem ipse non vulgaverit; sed amicos eius dictitavisse litteras Tiberii et mandata in Germanicum contineri, ac destinatum promere apud patres principemque arguere, ni elusus a Seiano per vana promissa foret; nec illum sponte exstinctum, verum immisso percussore. quorum neutrum adseveraverim; neque tamen occulere debui narratum ab iis qui nostram ad iuventam duraverunt. Caesar flexo in maestitiam ore suam invidiam tali morte quaesitam apud senatum . . . . . crebrisque interrogationibus exquirit qualem Piso diem supremum noctemque exegisset. atque illo pleraque sapienter quaedam inconsultius respondente, recitat codicillos a Pisone in hunc ferme modum compositos: "conspiratione inimicorum et invidia falsi criminis oppressus, quatenus veritati et innocentiae meae nusquam locus est, deos inmortalis testor vixisse me, Caesar, cum fide adversum te neque alia in matrem tuam pietate; vosque oro liberis meis consulatis, ex quibus Cn. Piso qualicumque fortunae meae non est adiunctus, cum omne hoc tempus in urbe egerit, M. Piso repetere Syriam dehortatus est.

109 **visum:** begins the indirect statement reporting the rumor Tacitus heard from his elders.

111 **dictitavisse:** introduces another indirect statement, reporting the assertions of Piso's friends. We are now in a rumor within a rumor.

113 **ni: nisi.**

Seiano: Sejanus was Tiberius's infamous right hand, the leader of the Praetorians.

115 **neutrum adseveraverim:** Skeptics might tend to disbelieve Tacitus here, asserting that his inclusion of this hearsay at all already displays a bias. What do you think? If Tacitus does have an ulterior motive for including this tale, what could it be?

116 **narratum:** Understand **id quod**, "what was related."

117 **flexo in maestitiam ore:** What do you think is the implication of Tacitus's choice of expression? What work is done by **flexo**?

suam invidiam ... quaesitam: indirect statement, though the verb governing it is lost in the lacuna. The subject is, however, clearly discernable as **Caesar**, thus: "Tiberius [said] before the senate that ill will against him was behind Piso's death." Tiberius apparently does not hesitate to betray the freshly dead Piso. It has been suggested that the lacuna here may be the corollary to the one above in section 14. In either case, more than a few words must be missing since the narrative picks back up with someone in Piso's household accounting for Piso's movements on the day before he was found dead.

120 **illo:** It is not clear who this is, perhaps one of Piso's sons, Gnaeus or Marcus. The subject of **recitat** cannot be same person, since **illo ... respondente** is an ablative absolute (A&G §419, note). It is likely the same subject as that of **exquirit**, perhaps Tiberius himself, who is the addressee of the **codicillos**.

122–23 **falsi criminis ... innocentiae meae:** Piso maintains his innocence even in his suicide note, though we should also keep in mind that the addressee is Tiberius, to whom Piso pledges his loyalty. It is interesting that, if indeed Tiberius and Livia instigated Germanicus's death, Piso does not allege this in the letter; on the other hand, surely Tiberius would not have read such a letter to the senate. It is useful to analyze Piso's rhetoric and political maneuvering in this his last action.

126 **consulatis:** here, "to consider favorably"; ablative absolute—**oro** is not used with the dative.

128 **repetere:** The understood accusative subject is **me**.

atque utinam ego potius filio iuveni quam ille patri seni
130 cessisset. eo impensius precor ne meae pravitatis poenas
innoxius luat. per quinque et quadraginta annorum
obsequium, per collegium consulatus, quondam divo
Augusto parenti tuo probatus et tibi amicus nec quicquam
post haec rogaturus salutem infelicis filii rogo." de Plancina
135 nihil addidit.

[17] post quae Tiberius adulescentem crimine civilis belli
purgavit, patris quippe iussa nec potuisse filium detrectare,
simul nobilitatem domus, etiam ipsius quoquo modo meriti
gravem casum miseratus. pro Plancina cum pudore et flagitio
140 disseruit, matris preces obtendens, in quam optimi cuiusque
secreti questus magis ardescebant. id ergo fas aviae
interfectricem nepotis adspicere, adloqui, eripere senatui.
quod pro omnibus civibus leges obtineant, uni Germanico
non contigisse. Vitellii et Veranii voce defletum Caesarem,
145 ab imperatore et Augusta defensam Plancinam. proinde
venena et artes tam feliciter expertas verteret in Agrippinam,
in liberos eius, egregiamque aviam ac patruum sanguine
miserrimae domus exsatiaret. biduum super hac imagine
cognitionis absumptum, urgente Tiberio liberos Pisonis
150 matrem uti tuerentur. et cum accusatores ac testes certatim
perorarent respondente nullo, miseratio quam invidia
augebatur.

130 **eo:** ablative of degree of difference with the comparative **impensius** (A&G §414.a).

pravitatis: On this count Piso admits guilt.

131-34 **per quinque ... rogo:** a rhetorically masterful final sentence from Piso, who pulls out all the stops: He cites his years of faithful service, his shared consulship with Tiberius, and the approval of Tiberius's adoptive father Augustus. On a more personal level, Piso also appeals to their friendship and to the fact that he will never again—obviously—ask anything of Tiberius. The rhetorical structure also builds to the final request: a TRICOLON, of which the first two are prepositional phrases (**per**) and the last is a participial clause. The final colon then expands into its own TRICOLON, **probatus ... amicus ... rogaturus**. The sentence ends with clear and simple syntax: **salutem infelicis filii rogo**.

134-35 **de Plancina nihil addidit:** a rhetorically masterful final sentence from Tacitus, as he observes that Piso has cut off his treacherous wife.

136 **adulescentem:** the younger son, Marcus.

civilis belli: in the province of Syria.

137 **patris quippe ... detrectare:** indirect statement.

138 **ipsius quoquo modo meriti:** because of its gender (**meriti**), must modify Piso, rather than **domus**.

141 **id ergo fas:** Understand **esse**; this begins the indirect statement that extends to **exsatiaret** alleging Plancina's crimes.

148-49 **hac imagine cognitionis:** "this sham investigation"; the ablative absolute **urgente Tiberio** provides the reason why the investigation was moot, namely that it was clear which side the emperor (and his mother) was on.

150 **matrem uti tuerentur: Matrem** is part of this indirect command; the subject of **tuerentur** is the **liberos Pisonis**.

150-51 **cum ... perorarent:** a **cum**-clause with a subjunctive verb: How might you translate this?

151 **respondente nullo:** because Piso is dead.

primus sententiam rogatus Aurelius Cotta consul (nam referente Caesare magistratus eo etiam munere fungebantur)
155 nomen Pisonis radendum fastis censuit, partem bonorum publicandam, pars ut Cn. Pisoni filio concederetur isque praenomen mutaret; M. Piso exuta dignitate et accepto quinquagies sestertio in decem annos relegaretur, concessa Plancinae incolumitate ob preces Augustae.

160 [18] multa ex ea sententia mitigata sunt a principe: ne nomen Pisonis fastis eximeretur, quando M. Antonii qui bellum patriae fecisset, Iulli Antonii qui domum Augusti violasset, manerent. et M. Pisonem ignominiae exemit concessitque ei paterna bona, satis firmus, ut saepe memoravi, adversum
165 pecuniam et tum pudore absolutae Plancinae placabilior. atque idem, cum Valerius Messalinus signum aureum in aede Martis Vltoris, Caecina Severus aram ultionis statuendam censuissent, prohibuit, ob externas ea victorias sacrari dictitans, domestica mala tristitia operienda. addiderat
170 Messalinus Tiberio et Augustae et Antoniae et Agrippinae Drusoque ob vindictam Germanici gratis agendas omiseratque Claudii mentionem. et Messalinum quidem L. Asprenas senatu coram percontatus est an prudens praeterisset; ac tum demum nomen Claudii adscriptum est.

153 **sententiam rogatus:** The verb is passive; verbs of asking in the passive can take an accusative (or two accusatives, if the verb is in the active voice) (A&G §396).

155 **fastis:** ablative of location or separation, "from the register of officeholders."

155-56 **partem ... pars:** Tacitus varies the indirect constructions: The first is accusative-infinitive indirect statement, while the second is a subjunctive noun clause. Gnaeus is asked to change his **praenomen** because his father (Gnaeus Calpurnius Piso) had the same. He changes it to Lucius.

157 **dignitate:** "senatorial rank."

158 **quinquagies sestertio:** Amounts greater than one million sesterces were expressed as the numeral adverb (ending in **-iens/ies**) with **sestertium**, with **sestertium** standing for one hundred thousand sesterces (A&G §634); thus **quinquagies sestertio** is five million sesterces, a sizeable sum of money, though M. Piso will have to make it last ten years.

relegaretur: As opposed to an **exsul**, whose property was confiscated, Piso will be allowed to keep his property. What do you think of these proposed punishments? Are they fitting, or too extreme?

multa ... a principe: Perhaps unsurprisingly, Tiberius rejects most of these proposals. What do you think of his decisions? What do you think Tacitus thinks?

162 **Iulli Antonii:** Mark Antony's son, who was executed by Augustus for having an affair with Augustus's daughter Julia (hence **domum ... violasset**).

166 **Valerius Messalinus:** father of Marcus Valerius, the consul of 20 CE, named in section 2 above. **Caecina Severus** was a commander of the army in Germania.

169 **tristitia:** ablative.

172 **Claudii:** Tiberius's brother, the future emperor Claudius, of Robert Graves's *I, Claudius* fame. He is regularly omitted from consideration and discussion because most believed his illness made him unsuitable for public office. Take note of how Tacitus writes of him here.

175 mihi quanto plura recentium seu veterum revolvo, tanto magis ludibria rerum mortalium cunctis in negotiis obversantur. quippe fama, spe, veneratione potius omnes destinabantur imperio quam quem futurum principem fortuna in occulto tenebat.

175 **mihi:** dative of person judging (A&G §378): "in my opinion."

Quanto ... tanto are correlative ablatives of degree of difference: "the more ... the more."

176 **ludibria:** Tacitus voices his cynicism at the folly and irony of human events, particularly in politics. **Quippe** in the next sentence is also a nice flavoring particle to Tacitus's foreshadowing of future events.

SUETONIUS

Tiberius 22–26, 33–36, 39–42
Higher Level Only

— Introduction to Suetonius —

Gaius Suetonius Tranquillus, like so many "Roman" authors, was born in the provinces and immigrated to Rome during his adult life. Though Suetonius was roughly ten years younger than Tacitus, the two men traveled in similar circles. He had a career in political and scholastic posts under Trajan and Hadrian, but he is most well known for his biographical output. Suetonius wrote several series of biographies (of poets, orators, and other famous figures), but only a few fragments of these have survived. Suetonius is now known chiefly for his biographies of emperors, *De vitis Caesarum*.

The Lives of the Caesars covers the twelve emperors from Julius Caesar to Domitian, who ruled during Suetonius's own time. Biography was considered an "inferior" subgenre of history as compared to Tacitus's annalistic histories, and indeed Suetonius's biographies contain a fair amount of titillating gossip about his subjects. The biographies typically begin by tracing the subject's family lineage, then moving chronologically through his youth, adult life, and reign. Toward the end of the biography, Suetonius devotes space to describe the personality, and particularly the appearance, of an emperor.

The selections here from the life of Tiberius treat some of the same personalities as the selections from Tacitus. Consider how the characterizations are similar and different.

— *Tiberius* 22–26 —

This selection provides some background into the dynamic between Tiberius and Germanicus. The year is 14 CE, and Augustus has just died. We find Tiberius seemingly hesitant to accept the emperorship, and Germanicus's popularity presents one of the obstacles for Tiberius.

[22] excessum Augusti non prius palam fecit, quam Agrippa iuvene interempto. hunc tribunus militum custos appositus occidit lectis codicillis, quibus ut id faceret iubebatur; quos codicillos dubium fuit, Augustusne moriens reliquisset, quo
5   materiam tumultus post se subduceret; an nomine Augusti Livia et ea conscio Tiberio an ignaro, dictasset. Tiberius renuntianti tribuno, factum esse quod imperasset, neque imperasse se et redditurum eum senatui rationem respondit, invidiam scilicet in praesentia vitans. nam mox silentio rem
10 obliteravit.

[23] iure autem tribuniciae potestatis coacto senatu incohataque adlocutione derepente velut impar dolori congemuit, utque non solum vox sed et spiritus deficeret optavit ac perlegendum librum Druso filio tradidit. inlatum
15 deinde Augusti testamentum, non admissis signatoribus nisi senatorii ordinis, ceteris extra curiam signa agnoscentibus, recitavit per libertum.

1   **excessum:** something of a EUPHEMISM: "death"; the subject of **fecit** is Tiberius.

1–2 **Agrippa iuvene:** Marcus Agrippa's son, born after his death and thus named Agrippa Postumus. He was adopted by Augustus after Agrippa Postumus's brothers Lucius and Gaius, prospective heirs of Augustus, died. But for unknown reasons he was exiled by Augustus to the small island of Planasia off the west coast of Italy.

SUETONIUS, *TIBERIUS* 22.1–23.17   49

3   **lectis codicillis:** ablative absolute, certainly not an ablative of instrument.

4   **Augustusne:** the first of two indirect questions (the second is **an nomine Augusti...**); **quo** introduces a relative clause of purpose (A&G §531.2).

6   **ea:** neuter plural.

    conscio Tiberio an ignaro: Suetonius suggests that Tiberius may have known about the execution order; the first sentence of this section reinforces this notion. **Dictasset** is the syncopated form of **dictavisset; imperasset** and **imperasse** are similarly syncopated—this is common in Suetonius.

7–8 **neque imperasse ... rationem:** Suetonius depicts this as a case of "the lady doth protest too much": Tiberius takes great pains to distance himself from the murder. **Se** is Tiberius, and **eum** is the unfortunate **tribunus** hung out to dry. By **redditurum ... senatui rationem** Tiberius means that he would haul the tribune before the senate for a trial.

8   **scilicet:** a colorful adverb reveals Suetonius's stance on Tiberius's actions.

11–12 **iure ... adlocutione:** lengthy scene-setting for the main action: two ablative absolutes (**coacto senatu** and **incohata adlocutione**), of which the first is modified by an ablative of means (**iure ... tribuniciae potestatis**). The **adlocutione** is the one announcing Augustus's death.

12 **velut impar dolori:** Suetonius again suggests that Tiberius is dissimulating.

13 **utque ... deficeret:** a subjunctive clause relating the contents of Tiberius's wish (**optavit**).

14 **non solum ... sed et:** "not only ... but also."

    Druso: Drusus the Younger, Tiberius's biological son; he was Tiberius's heir apparent until he died (he may have been poisoned) in 23 CE.

15 **testamentum:** object of **recitavit**.

testamenti initium fuit: "Quoniam atrox fortuna Gaium et
Lucium filios mihi eripuit, Tiberius Caesar mihi ex parte
dimidia et sextante heres esto." quo et ipso aucta suspicio est
opinantium successorem ascitum eum necessitate magis
quam iudicio, quando ita praefari non abstinuerit.

[24] principatum, quamvis neque occupare confestim
neque agere dubitasset, et statione militum, hoc est
vi et specie dominationis assumpta, diu tamen recusavit,
impudentissimo mimo nunc adhortantis amicos increpans ut
ignaros, quanta belua esset imperium, nunc precantem
senatum et procumbentem sibi ad genua ambiguis responsis
et callida cunctatione suspendens, ut quidam patientiam
rumperent atque unus in tumultu proclamaret: "Aut agat aut
desistat!" alter coram exprobraret ceteros, quod polliciti
sint tarde praestare, sed ipsum, quod praestet tarde polliceri.
tandem quasi coactus et querens miseram et onerosam
iniungi sibi servitutem, recepit imperium; nec tamen aliter,
quam ut depositurum se quandoque spem faceret. ipsius
verba sunt: "Dum veniam ad id tempus, quo vobis aequum
possit videri dare vos aliquam senectuti meae requiem."

20 **dimidia et sextante:** literally, "half and a sixth," which comes to
two-thirds.

esto: third person future imperative of **sum**, commonly used in formal documents (A&G §449.2).

quo ... ipso: to be taken together, referring to the statement from
Augustus's will.

21 **opinantium:** substantive use of the present participle, "of those
who thought," governing the indirect statement **successorem ...
abstinuerit**.

22	**quando ... abstinuerit: Quando** is used to report a reason asserted by the speaker (here, the **opinantium**); **abstinuerit**, in a dependent clause within indirect statement, is perfect subjunctive.
23–25	**quamvis ... assumpta:** The two adversative dependent clauses are stated differently: The first is **quamvis** with the subjunctive, the second is an ablative absolute, **statione ... assumpta**.
24	**statione:** "watch," "post," "guard."
26	**impudentissimo mimo:** Suetonius continues to criticize Tiberius for alleged dissimulation. What, according to Suetonius, is so offensive about Tiberius's behavior? **ut:** "as."
27	**Ignaros** introduces the indirect question **quanta ... imperium**. What does the characterization of the empire as a **belua** mean?
28	**sibi:** a dative of reference (A&G §377) referring back to Tiberius, the subject of the sentence.
29–30	**ut ... proclamaret:** result clause.
29	**quidam:** some of the senators.
30–31	**Aut agat aut desistat:** jussive subjunctives, appropriate for a short, exclamatory outburst.
31	**exprobraret:** introduces the indirect statement **ceteros ... polliceri**. Suetonius, in part because of the difference between annalistic history (e.g., Tacitus's *Annales*) and biography, includes more hearsay and gossip, particularly of the scandalous sort (as we will see below).
34	**servitutem:** Notice that Suetonius delays this word, separating it from its adjectives, thereby emphasizing it. How, then, is the word surprising? What does it mean for an emperor to complain about **servitus**? And what does it mean that Suetonius has composed this sentence in this way?
35	**ut ... faceret:** This entire noun clause is the comparison after **nec ... aliter quam**. Tiberius continues to pretend, in Suetonius's eyes, that he does not zealously covet the emperorship.
36	**Dum veniam: Dum** with the subjunctive implies intention or expectancy (A&G §553).
37	**senectuti:** Tiberius was indeed 65 years old when he acceded.

[25] cunctandi causa erat metus undique imminentium discriminum, ut saepe lupum se auribus tenere diceret. nam et servus Agrippae Clemens nomine non contemnendam manum in ultionem domini compararat et L. Scribonius Libo vir nobilis res novas clam moliebatur et duplex seditio militum in Illyrico et in Germania exorta est. flagitabant ambo exercitus multa extra ordinem, ante omnia ut aequarentur stipendio praetorianis. Germaniciani quidem etiam principem detractabant non a se datum summaque vi Germanicum, qui tum iis praeerat, ad capessendam rem p. urgebant, quanquam obfirmate resistentem. quem maxime casum timens, partes sibi quas senatui liberet, tuendas in re p. depoposcit, quando universae sufficere solus nemo posset nisi cum altero vel etiam cum pluribus. simulavit et valitudinem, quo aequiore animo Germanicus celerem successionem vel certe societatem principatus opperiretur. compositis seditionibus Clementem quoque fraude deceptum redegit in potestatem. Libonem, ne quid in novitate acerbius fieret, secundo demum anno in senatu coarguit, medio temporis spatio tantum cavere contentus;

38   **metus:** How does this word choice characterize Tiberius? What do you think Suetonius thinks of Tiberius? What word choices and phrases reveal Suetonius's characterization?

39   **lupum se auribus tenere:** a common idiom; **se** is the subject accusative, while **lupum** is the direct object. What do you think the idiom means? (There is a modern equivalent, "to have a tiger by the tail.")

40   **Non** is to be taken with **contemnendam** in a LITOTES of sorts.

41   **manum:** a "band of people," rather than "hand."
     in: "for" (A&G §221.12.1.c).

42	**res novas:** as in Tacitus *Annales* 3.13 above, "revolution," "uprising."
44	**ante omnia:** "before all," "above all."
44–45	**Ut ... praetorianis** is an indirect command following **flagitabant**.
45	**Germaniciani:** Germanicus's troops in Germany; their support, and Germanicus's popularity, made Germanicus a real threat to Tiberius, despite Germanicus's avowed disinterest in taking Tiberius's place.
47–48	**rem p.: rem publicam.**
49	**sibi:** refers back to the subject, Tiberius.
51	**simulavit:** in Suetonius's telling, a repeated tactic of Tiberius.
52	**valitudinem:** here, "bad health," "sickness."
52–53	**quo ... opperiretur:** relative clause of purpose. What is Tiberius's strategy here? Why does he think feigning sickness will placate Germanicus?
54	**compositis:** "reconcile," "settle," "arrange."
55	**quid: aliquid** after **ne**.
57	**tantum:** here, "only," "merely"; Tiberius may have taken some time to consolidate his power, but he nonetheless has systematically neutralized all threats to his rule. What does his strategy tell us about his style of political maneuvering?

nam et inter pontifices sacrificanti simul pro secespita
plumbeum cultrum subiciendum curavit et secretum petenti
non nisi adhibito Druso filio dedit dextramque obambulantis
veluti incumbens, quoad perageretur sermo, continuit.

[26] verum liberatus metu civilem admodum inter initia
ac paulo minus quam privatum egit. ex plurimis maximisque
honoribus praeter paucos et modicos non recepit. natalem
suum plebeis incurrentem circensibus vix unius bigae
adiectione honorari passus est. templa, flamines, sacerdotes
decerni sibi prohibuit, etiam statuas atque imagines nisi
permittente se poni; permisitque ea sola condicione, ne inter
simulacra deorum sed inter ornamenta aedium ponerentur.
intercessit et quo minus in acta sua iuraretur, et ne mensis
September Tiberius, October Livius vocarentur. praenomen
quoque imperatoris cognomenque patris patriae et civicam
in vestibulo coronam recusavit; ac ne Augusti quidem nomen,
quanquam hereditarium, ullis nisi ad reges ac dynastas
epistulis addidit. nec amplius quam mox tres consulatus,
unum paucis diebus, alterum tribus mensibus, tertium absens
usque in Idus Maias gessit.

58 **sacrificanti:** modifies an understood **Liboni**; so too with **petenti** and **obambulantis** (the latter is genitive). Why would Tiberius switch out Libo's sacrificial knife?

59 **secretum:** a meeting removed from the public eye: "a private interview."

60 **adhibito ... filio:** ablative absolute. Tiberius's precautions around Libo here foreshadow his suspicious and nearly paranoid nature, which would become increasingly prominent as his reign wore on.

62 **verum:** "but."

inter initia: "at the beginning"; notice that Suetonius foreshadows that Tiberius's behavior will be different later.

64–65 **natalem suum:** Understand **diem**: his birthday; **plebeis ... circensibus:** the chariot races at the Plebeian Games (**ludi plebeii**), which took place in mid-November. Tiberius's birthday was November 16.

68 **ea:** neuter plural; **sola** is ablative singular.

70 **intercessit:** "he prevented," anticipating both the **quo minus** clause and the negative purpose clause **ne ... vocarentur; iuraretur** is impersonal passive. **Livius** would have been after Tiberius's mother Livia.

73 **recusavit:** all of these honors and titles that Tiberius rejects were accepted by Julius Caesar, Augustus, or both, although the piling up of honors was not always well received. Tiberius may have had this in mind as he refused them, particularly as he used the title "Augustus" only when dealing with foreign rulers.

— *Tiberius* 33–36 —

Suetonius describes the early years of Tiberius's reign. As with other problematic emperors, Suetonius's assessment of Tiberius begins positively, cataloging his good characteristics and actions. These descriptions set the stage for the perversions Suetonius intends to unfurl later. Even at this early stage, we may detect— as surely Suetonius intends—indications of the idiosyncratic behavior to come.

[33] paulatim principem exseruit praestititque etsi varium diu, commodiorem tamen saepius et ad utilitates publicas proniorem. ac primo eatenus interveniebat, ne quid perperam fieret. itaque et constitutiones senatus quasdam rescidit et magistratibus pro tribunali cognoscentibus plerumque se offerebat consiliarium assidebatque iuxtim vel exadversum in parte primori; et si quem reorum elabi gratia rumor esset, subitus aderat iudicesque aut e plano aut e quaesitoris tribunali legum et religionis et noxae, de qua cognoscerent, admonebat; atque etiam, si qua in publicis moribus desidia aut mala consuetudine labarent, corrigenda suscepit.

[34] ludorum ac munerum impensas corripuit mercedibus scaenicorum recisis paribusque gladiatorum ad certum numerum redactis. Corinthiorum vasorum pretia in immensum exarsisse tresque mullos triginta milibus nummum venisse graviter conquestus, adhibendum supellectili modum censuit annonamque macelli senatus arbitratu quotannis temperandam, dato aedilibus negotio popinas ganeasque usque eo inhibendi, ut ne opera quidem pistoria proponi venalia sinerent. et ut parsimoniam publicam exemplo quoque iuvaret, sollemnibus ipse cenis pridiana saepe ac semesa obsonia apposuit dimidiatumque aprum, affirmans omnia eadem habere, quae totum.

cotidiana oscula edicto prohibuit, item strenarum
25 commercium ne ultra Kal. Ian. exerceretur. consuerat
quadriplam strenam, et de manu, reddere; sed offensus
interpellari se toto mense ab iis qui potestatem sui die festo
non habuissent, ultra non tulit.

3   **eatenus:** anticipates the clause **ne ... fieret**.

5   **pro tribunali:** The **tribunal** was a raised semicircular platform on which the magistrates would sit to hear cases. Tiberius would sit either among them or immediately before them.

7   **quem: aliquem** after **si**.

         Gratia is ablative, "by friendship," "by favor."

8–10   **aderat ... admonebat:** What does the use of the imperfect tense (as opposed to the perfect) tell us about these actions?

10–11   **si ... suscepit:** What kind of condition is this? How can the moods of the verb forms inform our understanding of the events they describe? Finally, based on this section, how might you describe Tiberius at this point in his emperorship? What do you take to be his concerns?

12   **munerum:** "gladiatorial shows."

13   **paribus:** "pairs."

16   **nummum:** genitive plural; another term for sesterce.

17   **annonam macelli:** "market prices."

19   **usque eo:** anticipates the result clause **ut ... sinerent**. How might you characterize Tiberius's restrictions in this paragraph?

24   **strenarum:** "New Year's gifts."

25   **Kal. Ian.:** the Kalends of January (January 1).

         exerceretur: indirect command without **ut** after **prohibuit**.

26   **de manu:** "in person."

27   **potestatem:** here, not "power," but "opportunity." What, according to Suetonius, is Tiberius's reason for halting the gift exchange precisely on January 1?

[35] matronas prostratae pudicitiae, quibus accusator
publicus deesset, ut propinqui more maiorum de communi
sententia coercerent auctor fuit. equiti Romano iuris
iurandi gratiam fecit, uxorem in stupro generi compertam
dimitteret, quam se numquam repudiaturum ante iuraverat.
feminae famosae, ut ad evitandas legum poenas iure
ac dignitate matronali exsolverentur, lenocinium profiteri
coeperant, et ex iuventute utriusque ordinis profligatissimus
quisque, quominus in opera scaenae harenaeque edenda
senatus consulto teneretur, famosi iudicii notam sponte
subibant; eos easque omnes, ne quod refugium in tali fraude
cuiquam esset, exsilio adfecit. senatori latum clavum ademit,
cum cognosset sub Kal. Iul. demigrasse in hortos, quo vilius
post diem aedes in urbe conduceret. alium e quaestura
removit, quod uxorem pridie sortitionem ductam postridie
repudiasset.

[36] externas caerimonias, Aegyptios Iudaicosque ritus
compescuit, coactis qui superstitione ea tenebantur
religiosas vestes cum instrumento omni comburere.
Iudaeorum iuventutem per speciem sacramenti in provincias
gravioris caeli distribuit, reliquos gentis eiusdem vel similia
sectantes urbe summovit, sub poena perpetuae servitutis nisi
obtemperassent. expulit et mathematicos, sed deprecantibus
ac se artem desituros promittentibus veniam dedit.

29 **matronas prostratae pudicitiae:** the direct object of the clause **ut
... coercerent**, which is dependent on the main clause **auctor fuit**.
Why do you think Suetonius positions the noun phrase not only first
in the sentence, but first in the paragraph?

32   **gratiam:** "excuse," "release."

33   **dimitteret:** imperfect subjunctive in a purpose clause without **ut**; the subject is the **eques**.

34–35 **ut ad evitandas legum poenas ... exsolverentur:** two purpose clauses, **ad** with the gerundive and **ut** with the subjunctive; read them as two parallel purpose clauses: "to avoid the punishments and to be released..."

Iure and **dignitate matronali** are ablatives of separation.

37   **in opera scaenae harenaeque edenda:** **In** here is "against"; **edenda** is from **edo, edere, edidi, editum**, "to produce," "to put forth."

38   **senatus consulto:** a decree of the senate prohibiting such behavior on the part of the nobles.

39   **refugium in tali fraude:** The profligate were finding loopholes that allowed them to practice their vices; Tiberius resolved the issue by simply exiling them.

40   **latum clavum:** the broad purple stripe on a senator's tunic.

41   **sub Kal. Iul.:** "before the Kalends of July," which was the first day of rentals. This senator moved out of the city so that he could secure a cheaper rate after the Kalends.

43   **quod:** here, "because."

sortitionem: a drawing by lot, for which his new wife gave him some advantage.

ductam: "married."

46   **coactis:** ablative absolute, taking the complementary infinitive **comburere**.

48   **sacramenti:** here, the military oath of allegiance.

50   **Urbe** is ablative of separation. With these last two paragraphs Suetonius begins to reveal how Tiberius's oversight of Roman **mores**, which began with an eye toward fairness, became increasingly narrow and punitive.

— *Tiberius* 39–42 —

This selection picks up in the year 26 CE, after the deaths of both Germanicus and Drusus. Tiberius's reclusive behavior begins to show itself, and Suetonius also takes the opportunity to report on some of Tiberius's more licentious hobbies.

[39] sed orbatus utroque filio, quorum Germanicus in Syria, Drusus Romae obierat, secessum Campaniae petit; constanti et opinione et sermone paene omnium quasi neque rediturus umquam et cito mortem etiam obiturus. quod paulo minus
5 utrumque evenit; nam neque Romam amplius rediit et paucos post dies iuxta Tarracinam in praetorio, cui Speluncae nomen est, incenante eo complura et ingentia saxa fortuito superne dilapsa sunt, multisque convivarum et ministrorum elisis praeter spem evasit.

10 [40] peragrata Campania, cum Capuae Capitolium, Nolae templum Augusti, quam causam profectionis praetenderat, dedicasset, Capreas se contulit, praecipue delectatus insula, quod uno parvoque litore adiretur, saepta undique praeruptis immensae altitudinis rupibus et profundo mari. statimque
15 revocante assidua obtestatione populo propter cladem, qua apud Fidenas supra viginti hominum milia gladiatorio munere amphitheatri ruina perierant, transiit in continentem potestatemque omnibus adeundi sui fecit; tanto magis, quod urbe egrediens ne quis se interpellaret edixerat ac toto itinere
20 adeuntis submoverat.

1 **Germanicus in Syria:** as detailed above, in Tacitus *Annales* 2.71. Drusus died in 23 CE under suspicious circumstances: He may have been poisoned. **Romae** is locative (A&G §43.c), as is **Campaniae**. **Campania** is an area south of Rome that includes the Bay of Naples

and the island of Capri. The subject of this sentence is Tiberius; for several years now he had taken to absenting himself from Rome, and after Drusus's death Tiberius leaves Rome in the hands of Sejanus, the head of the Praetorians. The ambitious Sejanus had plans for his own advancement and sought even to overthrow Tiberius in 31 CE; the plan was found out, and Sejanus was executed.

6 **Speluncae:** modern Sperlonga, just southeast of Tarracina. Tiberius had established a country home (**praetorium**) here, with a dining room built into a grotto (hence the town name **Spelunca**).

9 **praeter:** "against," "contrary to"; what does Suetonius tell us about Tiberius's popularity with the phrase **praeter spem**?

10 **Capuae ... Nolae:** both cities in Campania; **Capua** was then the dominant city in Campania.

12 **Capreas:** modern Capri; Tiberius would spend nearly the vast majority of the rest of his reign here; the accusative without the preposition **ad** is used of place names (A&G §427.2). Why does Tiberius choose this island? What does Suetonius aim to tell us about Tiberius's psychology from sharing these observations about Capri?

13 **quod:** "because."

Adiretur is potential subjunctive.

16 **apud Fidenas:** This amphitheater disaster, which takes place at the beginning of 27 CE, is described in more detail by Tacitus at *Annales* 4.62. The structure was apparently cheaply made and temporary; Tacitus reports that 50,000 spectators were injured.

18 **adeundi sui:** "of approaching him," "of having an audience with him."

tanto: ablative of degree of difference.

Quod is "because" here.

19 **Se** refers to the subject of the entire sentence, Tiberius.

[41] regressus in insulam rei p. quidem curam usque adeo abiecit, ut postea non decurias equitum umquam suppleverit, non tribunos militum praefectosque, non provinciarum praesides ullos mutaverit, Hispaniam et Syriam per aliquot
25 annos sine consularibus legatis habuerit, Armeniam a Parthis occupari, Moesiam a Dacis Sarmatisque, Gallias a Germanis vastari neglexerit; magno dedecore imperii nec minore discrimine.

[42] ceterum secreti licentiam nanctus et quasi civitatis oculis
30 remotis, cuncta simul vitia male diu dissimulata tandem profudit; de quibus singillatim ab exordio referam. in castris tiro etiam tum propter nimiam vini aviditatem pro Tiberio "Biberius," pro Claudio "Caldius," pro Nerone "Mero" vocabatur. postea princeps in ipsa publicorum morum
35 correctione cum Pomponio Flacco et L. Pisone noctem continuumque biduum epulando potandoque consumpsit, quorum alteri Syriam provinciam, alteri praefecturam urbis confestim detulit, codicillis quoque iucundissimos et omnium horarum amicos professus. Cestio Gallo, libidinoso
40 ac prodigo seni, olim ab Augusto ignominia notato et a se ante paucos dies apud senatum increpito cenam ea lege condixit, ne quid ex consuetudine immutaret aut demeret, utque nudis puellis ministrantibus cenaretur.

21 **rei p.:** as above at section 25, **rei publicae.**
23–27 **ut...neglexerit:** The rest of the paragraph details some of the state duties neglected by Tiberius and the resulting consequences of his neglect.
29 **ceterum:** "but."

31 **de quibus singillatim ab exordio referam:** The reporting of such dirty laundry is a hallmark of Suetonius's biographical style. It is not, however, merely for titillation: Suetonius believes that psychological and personal analysis are important components of a political profile. Thus he also devotes space in his biographies for descriptions of his subjects' facial and bodily characteristics, which he often associates with personality traits.

33 **Biberius:** a play on the verb **bibo**; **Caldius:** from **calidum**, a hot drink made of warmed wine and water; **Mero:** from **merum**, unmixed wine. Each of these nicknames rhymes with part of his pre-adoption name, Tiberius Claudius Nero.

34–35 **in ipsa publicorum morum correctione:** Suetonius points out Tiberius's hypocrisy: It is not only that Tiberius prevents the merry-making of others, but that he engages in it himself to excess.

38–39 **iucundissimos et omnium horarum amicos:** In addition to hypocrisy, Tiberius seems also to be guilty of cronyism. **omnium horarum:** "ready," "well-disposed at all times." The men mentioned in this section are not well known outside of their mention here.

41 **ea lege:** namely, the indirect commands that follow this clause.

42 **condixit:** "attended."

43 **nudis puellis ministrantibus:** yet another aspect of Tiberius's alleged licentious behavior to add to drinking, eating, and cronyism.

ignotissimum quaesturae candidatum nobilissimis anteposuit
45 ob epotam in convivio propinante se vini amphoram. Asellio Sabino sestertia ducenta donavit pro dialogo, in quo boleti et ficedulae et ostreae et turdi certamen induxerat. novum denique officium instituit a voluptatibus, praeposito equite R. T. Caesonio Prisco.

44 **ignotissimum . . . nobilissimis:** Suetonius uses two superlatives in close proximity to emphasize the disparity between the man who was given the post and the ones who deserved it.

45 **propinante se:** ablative absolute; **se** refers to the subject of the sentence, Tiberius. Once again, the offenses are multiplied: Not only does Tiberius prefer the less qualified candidate, he does so because of a drinking bet.

46 **sestertia ducenta:** 200,000 sesterces, a not insignificant amount of money for what seems a laughable composition.

48 **a voluptatibus:** indeed, the theme of this entire section, namely, that Tiberius was more devoted to pleasures of the body than he feigned. Suetonius also suggests in this section that Tiberius's judgment was questionable, as he takes actions that are flagrantly and patently wasteful or ridiculous.

Sestertius (Photograph by Rama, Wikimedia Commons, Cc-by-sa-2.0-fr)

The *sestertius*, during the Roman Republic a silver coin, was minted in brass during Imperial times. This *sestertius*, produced around 176 CE, features a portrait of the emperor Marcus Aurelius. Under the emperors, coins often depicted a portrait of the current emperor on the obverse (front); the reverse (back) varied widely.

— *Tiberius* 52–53 —

These sections illustrate Tiberius's relationships with Germanicus, Agrippina, and Drusus. Suetonius gives us insight into Tiberius's psychology through his interactions with his family.

[52] filiorum neque naturalem Drusum neque adoptivum Germanicum patria caritate dilexit, alterius vitiis infensus. nam Drusus fluxioris remissiorisque vitae erat. itaque ne mortuo quidem perinde adfectus est, sed tantum non statim
5   a funere ad negotiorum consuetudinem rediit iustitio longiore inhibito. quin et Iliensium legatis paulo serius consolantibus, quasi obliterata iam doloris memoria, irridens se quoque respondit vicem eorum dolere, quod egregium civem Hectorem amisissent. Germanico usque adeo
10 obtrectavit, ut et praeclara facta eius pro supervacuis elevarit et gloriosissimas victorias ceu damnosas rei p. increparet. quod vero Alexandream propter immensam et repentinam famem inconsulto se adisset, questus est in senatu. etiam causa mortis fuisse ei per Cn. Pisonem legatum Syriae
15 creditur, quem mox huius criminis reum putant quidam mandata prolaturum, nisi ea secreto ostentanti auferenda ipsumque iugulandum curasset. propter quae multifariam inscriptum et per noctes celeberrime adclamatum est: "Redde Germanicum!" quam suspicionem confirmavit ipse
20 postea coniuge etiam ac liberis Germanici crudelem in modum afflictis.

2   **alterius:** the former, Drusus.
3–4   **ne mortuo quidem:** How does Suetonius characterize Tiberius, based on his description of Tiberius's relationship with his sons?

6   **quin:** "but."

Iliensium: Ilium, a.k.a. Troy.

7   **quasi . . . memoria:** ablative absolute, as is **Iliensium . . . consolantibus.**

7–8   **irridens . . . respondit:** The subject is Tiberius.

8   **vicem:** "fate," "lot."

quod: "that."

9   **Hectorem:** Consider Tiberius's choice of example: Hector was not a recent historical figure, like Drusus, but a long-dead mythological figure. What does the disjointed nature of his reply tell us about Tiberius's frame of mind?

Germanico: Obtrectavit takes the dative. Tiberius's relationship with Germanicus is the polar opposite of the one with Tiberius: He despises Drusus for, frankly, sharing the same vices he does and denigrates Germanicus for excelling.

13   **inconsulto:** This element seems rather to have been what angered Tiberius the most, that he could not share in the glory of Germanicus's magnanimity.

14   **ei:** Germanicus; the subject of **creditur** is Tiberius. Suetonius here reports the same rumors about Germanicus's death that Tacitus reports at 3.16.

16   **mandata:** substantive, "commands," "orders."

Prolaturum modifies the **reum** Piso.

secreto ostentanti: dative of agent with passive periphrastic **ea . . . auferenda** (A&G §374).

18   **inscriptum . . . et . . . adclamatum est:** The subject is the quotation that follows, **"Redde Germanicum!"** Compare Suetonius's and Tacitus's (2.82–83) descriptions of the aftermath of Germanicus's death.

19   **ipse:** Tiberius.

[53] nurum Agrippinam post mariti mortem liberius
quiddam questam manu apprehendit Graecoque versu: "Si
non dominaris," inquit, "filiola, iniuriam te accipere
25　existimas?" nec ullo mox sermone dignatus est. quondam
vero inter cenam porrecta a se poma gustare non ausam
etiam vocare desiit, simulans veneni se crimine accersi; cum
praestructum utrumque consulto esset, ut et ipse temptandi
gratia offerret et illa quasi certissimum exitium caveret.
30　novissime calumniatus modo ad statuam Augusti modo ad
exercitus confugere velle, Pandatariam relegavit
conviciantique oculum per centurionem verberibus excussit.
rursus mori inedia destinanti per vim ore diducto infulciri
cibum iussit. sed et perseverantem atque ita absumptam
35　criminosissime insectatus, cum diem quoque natalem eius
inter nefastos referendum suasisset, imputavit etiam, quod
non laqueo strangulatam in Gemonias abiecerit; proque
tali clementia interponi decretum passus est, quo sibi gratiae
agerentur et Capitolino Iovi donum ex auro sacraretur.

23　**quiddam:** direct object of **questam**.

24　**dominaris:** Tiberius's insensitivity to Agrippina's loss adds to Suetonius's depiction of Tiberius and Germanicus. Notice the somewhat patronizing tone of the DIMINUTIVE **filiola**: it could have been meant, and taken, as both a sign of sympathy and—as Suetonius likely does—as mock politeness, that is, being polite, but ironically.

27　**simulans:** Once again, dissimulation is showcased as Tiberius's primary characteristic; but, as both Tacitus and Suetonius suggest, Agrippina may not be entirely wrong to worry about being poisoned by Tiberius.

28-29　**temptandi gratia:** Why do you think Tiberius tests Agrippina? What did he have to gain by it?

30 **modo ... modo:** "now ... now," "sometimes ... sometimes"; consider Agrippina's choice of places to seek refuge: Why would these objects or people be well disposed toward her?

31 **Pandatariam relegavit:** Pandataria: an island off the western coast of Italy, just northwest of the Bay of Naples; Agrippina, like Marcus Piso above at Tacitus *Annales* 3.17, is **relegata**, not an **exsul**.

32 **convicianti:** substantive use of the present participle, referring to Agrippina: "the one who was complaining"; a dative of reference, verging on a dative of possession (A&G §376–77, 373). Suetonius here showcases, obviously, Tiberius's cruelty.

33 **destinanti:** present participle used substantively, in the dative; it refers to Agrippina, as do **perseverantem** and **absumptam**.

37 **Gemonias:** as above at Tacitus *Annales* 3.14, the steps off of which the bodies of executed criminals were thrown into the Tiber River.

38 **passus est:** no doubt sarcastic, as if Agrippina deserved to be treated like a criminal. In return for his outrageous treatment of Agrippina (he did drive her to suicide), Tiberius is publicly thanked, and a golden gift is dedicated in his honor. Consider Tiberius's liberality in the use of state funds in comparison with his earlier abstemiousness.

Good Living

Portrait of Epicurus.
Late 3rd–early 2nd century BCE,
Roman copy after a lost Hellenistic original.
(Wikimedia Commons)

Epicurus (341–270 BCE) was a Greek philosopher who studied atomist philosophy with followers of Democritus before moving to Athens and starting his own school of philosophy, Epicureanism. Though Epicurus was a prolific writer, most of his works are now lost. In addition to the remaining three letters by Epicurus, later Epicurean philosophers, including Lucretius, are now the primary source of knowledge about his teachings.

Introduction to Good Living

In the passages that follow, various Roman authors (Lucretius, Horace, and Seneca) consider the age-old question, "What is the meaning of life?" They think about what is worthy of our time and effort, and what is not, given the brevity of human life and its vicissitudes. What is happiness, and how is it achieved? As representatives of Epicureanism (Lucretius, Horace) and Stoicism (Seneca), the three authors have differing beliefs about what causes events to transpire: Epicureans believe that everything happens by cause and effect, while the Stoics believe in fate. Nonetheless, both philosophies recognize the importance of choice, tranquillity, and a sense of self-control for living a happy life.

Questions about how to live one's life are just as relevant to us today as they were back then. I would encourage you, then, to read these passages not only as an academic exercise in Latin literature, but as advice from friends who just might have something useful to say about how you live your life. Engage with the material; try to see what their advice means for you, in your life; argue with them if you don't agree.

Before you begin reading, consider how you would answer these questions:

- What makes you happy? Really happy?
- What ruins your day? Why does it ruin your day? How does it make you feel?
- What did you spend a lot of time on recently? Why did you spend so much time on it? Was it worth it?
- What do you want to do with your life? Why?

LUCRETIUS

De Rerum Natura 1.54–135; 2.1–61 (SL and HL)
Standard Level and Higher Level

— Introduction to Lucretius —

Interest in Lucretius has experienced a revival in recent years, as a wave of scholarship explored Lucretius's influence on early modern literature and culture. The affinities between Epicurean physics and our contemporary understanding of physics, particularly the atom, have long been recognized. Thus Lucretius has always held allure for readers.

De Rerum Natura (*DRN*) seeks, in six books of dactylic poetry, to describe Epicurean physics and its consequences in Epicurean ethics. Epicurus was a Greek philosopher who was just a few decades younger than Aristotle. At the peaceful Epicurean Garden away from the bustling city center of Athens, Epicurus taught his philosophy of atomism and freedom from pain. Though Epicurus was a prolific writer, we now have but three of his letters remaining. Lucretius thus takes the raw material available in what remained to him of Epicurus's writings and adapts it into Latin, and into verse. The choice of dactylic hexameter is intentional: The meter is used for didactic (from Greek *didasko*, "to teach") poetry—the *DRN*'s predecessors include Hesiod's *Works and Days* and Parmenides's *On Nature*. These poems seek to teach their readers about farming, philosophy, or, more broadly, how to live a good life. While the notion of putting advice into poetic form may seem strange to us at first, we might compare it to our modern poetic forms like the haiku, or even poetic statements like fortune cookie aphorisms. Since the *DRN* is in meter, it is important to scan the lines, not only for grammatical purposes, but also to appreciate the poetic artistry.

Epicureans were strict materialists, believing that everything in the universe was made of matter. All events, therefore, were a result of the interaction of matter, rather than the workings of fate or the gods. While Lucretius does concede the existence of gods, they are to him perfect beings who would not mar their perfection with human interaction. Accordingly Lucretius believes that human unhappiness derives not from bad fate, but from ignorance and mistaken beliefs. Since Epicureans hold that happiness is achieved through increasing pleasure and decreasing pain, Lucretius finds that ignorance of the workings of the world ought to be dispelled.

About Lucretius's own life we know very little. His full name was Titus Lucretius Carus, and he was born around 100 BCE and died between 50 and 40 BCE. The *DRN* would thus have been written during the last days of the Roman Republic. St. Jerome has recorded two rather dubious stories about Lucretius's life: (1) that Cicero posthumously edited the *DRN*; (2) that Lucretius wrote the *DRN* while in the throes of a love potion. The latter claim is certainly false; the former is very likely untrue.

— Meter —

Dactylic Hexameter

Athenian agora (Wikimedia Commons)

Both the Epicurean and Stoic schools were founded in Athens. The Stoics were named for the building in which they met, the *Stoa Poikile* in the agora. The agora was a commercial, political, and religious center. In antiquity, the agora was severely damaged and was rebuilt several times. The Acropolis, home to the famous Parthenon, is visible in the background.

— *De Rerum Natura* 1.54–79 —

In this first selection, Lucretius lays out his philosophical program and praises Epicurus, the founder of the Epicurean school of thought. As Lucretius sees it, understanding the fundamental material basis for the world will prevent us from being oppressed by superstition and unfounded beliefs.

    nam tibi de summa caeli ratione deumque
55 disserere incipiam et rerum primordia pandam,
    unde omnis natura creet res auctet alatque
    quove eadem rursum natura perempta resolvat,
    quae nos materiem et genitalia corpora rebus
    reddunda in ratione vocare et semina rerum
60 appellare suemus et haec eadem usurpare
    corpora prima, quod ex illis sunt omnia primis.
    humana ante oculos foede cum vita iaceret
    in terris oppressa gravi sub religione
    quae caput a caeli regionibus ostendebat
65 horribili super aspectu mortalibus instans,

54   **tibi:** Lucretius's addressee is likely Gaius Memmius Gemellus, a Roman politician in the republican period. As with much of didactic literature, the poem is explicitly addressed to one person but is meant for wider readership. The direct addressee stands in for the reader and allows the poet to address the reader directly using the second person singular. Thus the reader may feel as if she or he is being directly spoken to.

        ratione: As often in Lucretius, **ratio** refers to the logic or organizational structure that underpins the entire world. As we will see, Epicureanism has a very materialistic, and arguably mechanistic, understanding of how the world works and events happen.

        deum[que]: the syncopated form of **deorum**.

55   **incipiam ... pandam:** future active indicatives.

56   **creet[que] ... auctet alat:** These verbs and those that follow are subjunctives in indirect questions introduced by **unde** and **quove** (line 57). The two clauses work in tandem, referring to the process of creation and disintegration.

58   **materiem et genitalia corpora:** Along with **semina** (line 59) and **corpora prima** (line 61), these terms refer to the primary building blocks of the universe. We are nowadays accustomed to call them atoms; while Lucretius (and his predecessors Epicurus and Democritus) provides descriptions that are strikingly similar to modern atomic theory, we should be careful not to assimilate all of his explanations to our modern understanding of physics. We can, however, extrapolate from these terms that what Lucretius envisions are small particles that form the fundamental underlying matter of our world: They are generative (**genitalia**) and the seeds (**semina**) of objects. Moreover, they are firmly sensible objects (**corpora**); we can contrast his materialistic understanding of the composition of the universe with other philosophies, which grant greater prominence to the importance of form, ideas, and abstract notions in the composition of the world.

59   **reddunda:** archaic form of **reddenda**.

61   **quod:** here, "because."

62   **cum ... iaceret:** circumstantial **cum**-clause that extends, with participial clauses and a relative clause, through **instans** in line 65 (A&G §545).

63   **gravi sub religione:** Lucretius views religion as the source of much unhappiness in society. As he explains below, people perform heinous acts under the compulsion of the gods; he also faults religion for the overwhelming fear of death that paralyzes humans. Are there similar debates about religion in the modern world?

65   **super:** the adverb, here.

   Instans takes the dative.

primum Graius homo mortalis tollere contra
est oculos ausus primusque obsistere contra,
quem neque fama deum nec fulmina nec minitanti
murmure compressit caelum, sed eo magis acrem
70 irritat animi virtutem, effringere ut arta
naturae primus portarum claustra cupiret.
ergo vivida vis animi pervicit, et extra
processit longe flammantia moenia mundi
atque omne immensum peragravit mente animoque,
75 unde refert nobis victor quid possit oriri,
quid nequeat, finita potestas denique cuique
quanam sit ratione atque alte terminus haerens.
quare religio pedibus subiecta vicissim
obteritur, nos exaequat victoria caelo.

66 **primum:** adverb.

Graius homo: Epicurus. Lucretius begins fully half of the books (3, 5, and 6) with praise of Epicurus; where one typically expects an invocation to the Muse or a deity (as in Book 1, which begins with an invocation to Venus), Lucretius writes in praise of the mortal who denounced stories of the gods. The *i* of **mortalis** is long: accusative plural. Nonetheless Lucretius places it next to **Graius homo**.

contra: Both this line and the next end with the same word. This was certainly intentional: Why might Lucretius have wanted to call attention to this word?

67 **est ... ausus:** The two parts of the perfect passive construction have been separated.

68 **deum: deorum**, as above at line 54.

69 **eo magis:** "so much more"; ablative of degree of difference with a comparative (A&G §414).

70 **irritat:** The final syllable is long; it is thus the syncopated form of **irritavit**.

70–71　**ut ... cupiret:** result clause following **eo magis** above (line 69). Notice the CHIASTIC word order of this clause even as it ENJAMBS over the line break: **arta naturae primus portarum claustra**. Epicurus (**primus**), of course, takes pride of place in the center of the clause as he forces his way through the doors.

72　**vivida vis ... pervicit:** Read this line aloud and notice the ALLITERATION of "*v*."

72–73　**extra processit ... :** a vivid and striking image of Epicurus striding beyond the boundaries of our world through the force of his mind.

74　**Omne** is here substantive: "the universe," "everything."

75　**refert nobis victor:** a METAPHOR, comparing Epicurus to a triumphant Roman general returning with spoils of war. The spoils are, specifically, knowledge of the natural world (here phrased in the form of indirect questions).

76–77　**finita ... ratione:** the third indirect question, after relating what does (indirect question #1) and does not (#2) exist: finally (**denique**) the natural laws that govern what does exist. **Quanam ratione** is the interrogative.

77　**alte terminus haerens:** a METAPHOR: The **terminus** is a stone that marks the boundary line between two properties. It clings (**haerens**) deeply (**alte**), just like the laws of nature.

— *De Rerum Natura* 1.80–101 —

In this section, Lucretius describes at length an example of the evil performed for the sake of religion: Agamemnon's sacrifice of his daughter, Iphigenia, to appease the goddess Diana (Artemis).

80 illud in his rebus vereor, ne forte rearis
    impia te rationis inire elementa viamque
    indugredi sceleris. quod contra saepius illa
    religio peperit scelerosa atque impia facta.
    Aulide quo pacto Triviai virginis aram
85 Iphianassai turparunt sanguine foede
    ductores Danaum delecti, prima virorum.
    cui simul infula virgineos circumdata comptus
    ex utraque pari malarum parte profusast,
    et maestum simul ante aras adstare parentem
90 sensit et hunc propter ferrum celare ministros
    aspectuque suo lacrimas effundere civis,
    muta metu terram genibus summissa petebat.
    nec miserae prodesse in tali tempore quibat
    quod patrio princeps donarat nomine regem.

80   **ne . . . rearis:** fear clause following **vereor** (A&G §564). Notice the second person address, which brings the reader into the poem; Lucretius anticipates Memmius's/the reader's anxieties about impiety.

82   **indugredi:** archaic form for **ingredi**.

  contra: the adverb here, rather than the preposition.

84   **Aulide:** locative, "at Aulis."

  Quo pacto means "in this manner," and Lucretius uses it to introduce an example of his assertion.

  Triviai is archaic feminine genitive singular, modifying **virginis**; the phrase refers to Diana (Artemis), the goddess of the crossroads (**trivia**).

85 **Iphianassai:** another archaic genitive singular form; Lucretius uses **Iphianassa** for Iphigenia. As most famously told in Euripides's *Iphigenia in Aulis*, Agamemnon sacrificed his daughter so that the Greek fleet could gain favorable winds and set sail for Troy. Iphigenia was brought to Aulis under false pretenses, that she was to be wed to Achilles; she only belatedly realizes the real reason.

86 **Danaum:** the Danaans, a term for the Greeks; this form is masculine genitive plural. **Prima**, although neuter plural, also refers to the **ductores**.

87 **cui:** refers to Iphigenia.

simul: simul ac, "as soon as."

infula: Compare with **vitta**. An **infula** is worn by a sacrificial victim, whereas a **vitta** can also be worn by a bride. What does Lucretius's word choice mean?

Comptus is the accusative direct object, of sorts, of the passive participle **circumdata**—similar to the hyperspecific "accusative of body part" (A&G §397b–c): "placed around her hair."

88 **profusast:** elision of **profusa est**.

89 **parentem:** Agamemnon; **hunc** in the next line also refers to him.

90 **sensit:** The subject is Iphigenia, who now recognizes what is about to happen to her.

propter: in the more physical sense here: "next to"; its object, **hunc**, precedes it.

92 **muta metu:** Notice the touching ALLITERATION: What effect do you think it has?

93 **quibat:** shortened form of **quiebat**, from **queo**, "to be able"; the subject of the verb is the **quod**-clause of the next line.

94 **princeps donarat:** Both modify Iphigenia; **donarat** is the syncopated form for **donaverat**.

Regem is, of course, Agamemnon.

95 nam sublata virum manibus tremibundaque ad aras
    deductast, non ut sollemni more sacrorum
    perfecto posset claro comitari Hymenaeo,
    sed casta inceste nubendi tempore in ipso
    hostia concideret mactatu maesta parentis,
100 exitus ut classi felix faustusque daretur.
    tantum religio potuit suadere malorum.

95   **virum:** syncopated form for **virorum**.
96   **deductast:** elision for **deducta est**.
     ut ... posset ... concideret: purpose clauses.
97   **Hymenaeo:** the wedding song, in honor of the god Hymen.
98   **casta inceste:** The JUXTAPOSITION of opposing terms underscores Iphigenia's innocence and, as Lucretius sees it, the crime of religion in imposing this killing. The nouns and adjectives interspersed throughout these lines to describe Iphigenia also reiterate the point: **casta**, **hostia** (line 99), **maesta** (line 99).
100 **ut ... daretur:** purpose clause. Lucretius intentionally uses **felix** and **faustus** ironically, to mock the notion that one would derive good fortune from the death of an innocent maiden.
101 **malorum:** partitive genitive with **tantum**.

The sacrifice of Iphigenia (Wikimedia Commons)

Two men carry Iphigenia (center) to be sacrificed. Agamemnon (left) covers his face in grief while the seer Calchas (right) looks on. In this version of the tale, Artemis (Diana) appears with a hind that will be sacrificed in place of Iphigenia. This fresco was found in a villa in Pompeii.

— *De Rerum Natura* 1.102–26 —

Lucretius expands on his criticism of religion: Religion has taught us to fear death, because we fear what is claimed to come after death, i.e., the Underworld. This section concludes with a revision of his earlier "table of contents" (1.54–57).

    tutemet a nobis iam quovis tempore vatum
    terriloquis victus dictis desciscere quaeres.
    quippe etenim quam multa tibi iam fingere possunt
105 somnia quae vitae rationes vertere possint
    fortunasque tuas omnis turbare timore!
    et merito. nam si certam finem esse viderent
    aerumnarum homines, aliqua ratione valerent
    religionibus atque minis obsistere vatum.
110 nunc ratio nulla est restandi, nulla facultas,
    aeternas quoniam poenas in morte timendumst.
    ignoratur enim quae sit natura animai,
    nata sit an contra nascentibus insinuetur,
    et simul intereat nobiscum morte dirempta
115 an tenebras Orci visat vastasque lacunas
    an pecudes alias divinitus insinuet se,

102   **tutemet:** emphatic form of **tu**; notice its important placement at the beginning of the line.

       a nobis: Take with **desciscere** (line 103), not **quaeres** (line 103).

       Vatum, genitive plural, is ENJAMBED and modifies **terriloquis victus dictis** (line 103).

104   **quam:** an exclamation, "how!" The subject of **possunt** are the **vates** from two lines above.

105   **possint:** subjunctive in a relative clause of characteristic (A&G §535). These prophets are able, with mere talk, to incite terrifying visions and scare us into submission.

107 **et merito:** an example of Lucretius's rhetorical dialogic style. He often imagines the positions of interlocutors and replies to them; here, he affirms and recognizes the fear of his interlocutor, but he will immediately turn around and attempt to disabuse Memmius of his misperceptions about the gods.

Finem is a EUPHEMISM for death.

Valerent takes another infinitive (**obsistere**) and is meant here as "to be strong enough to," "to be able to."

107-108 **viderent ... valerent:** imperfect subjunctives in a present subjunctive (contrary-to-fact) condition (A&G §517).

111 **timendumst:** Contraction for **timendum est**; it is here impersonal ("there needs to be feared," "one needs to fear") and takes **aeternas ... poenas** as its direct object. As Lucretius sees it, religion causes humans to fear death because it propagates stories of the soul suffering eternal damnation after death. He will proceed to refute that the soul has an afterlife.

112 **ignoratur:** The indirect question **quae sit natura animai** is the subject. **Animai** is the archaic genitive singular.

113 **nata sit:** subjunctive in indirect question; understand **utrum**. This **utrum ... an contra** dichotomy parses the previous indirect question about the nature of the soul: whether a baby is born with the soul or the soul makes its way into a newborn from elsewhere.

114-16 **intereat ... visat ... insinuet:** continuation of the indirect questions inquiring into the nature of the soul, this time offering three possible outcomes at death: (1) it dies with the body; (2) it survives and goes to the Underworld; (3) it is reincarnated into another being. Epicureans adopt the first belief; the second belongs to religion; the third is adopted, perhaps most famously, by the Pythagoreans, who were consequently vegetarians.

Ennius ut noster cecinit qui primus amoeno
detulit ex Helicone perenni fronde coronam,
per gentis Italas hominum quae clara clueret;
120 etsi praeterea tamen esse Acherusia templa
Ennius aeternis exponit versibus edens,
quo neque permaneant animae neque corpora nostra,
sed quaedam simulacra modis pallentia miris;
unde sibi exortam semper florentis Homeri
125 commemorat speciem lacrimas effundere salsas
coepisse et rerum naturam expandere dictis.

117 **Ennius ut noster cecinit:** Ennius was an epic poet, regarded as the Roman Homer. Very little of his work survives, but he was notable as the first to apply Greek meters (**amoeno ex Helicone**, lines 117–18) to Roman poetry.

118 **Helicone:** a mountain in Greece, the mythical home of the Muses who inspire poetry.

perenni fronde coronam: METAPHORICAL, representing poetic renown.

120 **esse:** existential **est**, "that there are"; **Acherusia** refers to the river Acheron, which flowed through the Underworld.

122 **quo:** There is some disagreement among scholars whether to take **quo** as "where" or "to where"; Lucretius does not mean to say that souls and bodies are torn apart in the Underworld; rather he means that neither reach the Underworld because they are dissipated.

123 **quaedam simulacra ... pallentia:** Ennius believed in an Underworld, but he believed that neither souls nor bodies abided there—only dim phantoms.

125 **commemorat:** subject is Ennius; it governs the indirect statement, which in prose would more likely be ordered **speciem ... coepisse ... effundere**.

— *De Rerum Natura* 1.127–35 —

quapropter bene cum superis de rebus habenda
nobis est ratio, solis lunaeque meatus
qua fiant ratione, et qua vi quaeque gerantur
130 in terris, tunc cum primis ratione sagaci
unde anima atque animi constet natura videndum,
et quae res nobis vigilantibus obvia mentis
terrificet morbo adfectis somnoque sepultis,
cernere uti videamur eos audireque coram,
135 morte obita quorum tellus amplectitur ossa.

127–35 **nobis ... ossa:** The following section is known as the "second syllabus" (the "first syllabus" being the initial table of contents at lines 54–57), wherein Lucretius refines his list of topics to cover in the *DRN*. In this revision he lists the topics of meteorology (the topic of Book 5), terrestrial phenomena (covered in Books 5–6), the nature of the mind and soul (Book 3), and visions, real or imagined (Book 4).

127 **cum:** with **tunc** (line 130), "not only ... but also," "both ... and."

superis de rebus: The adjective precedes the preposition.

130 **cum primis:** "and especially."

131 **unde:** introduces an indirect question governed by **videndum (est)**, for which the verb is **constet**. Lucretius defines the difference between **anima** and **animus** in Book 3: The former is akin to "breath," the force that animates us, while the latter is akin to "mind," the intellectual capacity.

132 **quae res:** In Book 4 Lucretius discusses **simulacra** and how (he believes) vision works. This involves the expulsion of thin films or sheets of atoms from objects, which thence reach our eyeballs to produce vision. Hallucinations and dreams, as he sees it, are remnants of these atoms in our eyes. **Mentis** is poetic accusative plural for **mentes**.

134 **uti:** ut, introducing a result clause: another consequence of hallucinations.

— *De Rerum Natura* 2.1–61 —

In this opening passage to Book 2, Lucretius argues for the value of philosophy. Although most people strive for money, power, and fame, he asserts that these possessions will not, at the end of the day, make us happy. The things that make us happy, he claims, are few in number and easily enough acquired.

       suave, mari magno turbantibus aequora ventis,
       e terra magnum alterius spectare laborem;
       non quia vexari quemquamst iucunda voluptas,
       sed quibus ipse malis careas quia cernere suave est.
6   suave etiam belli certamina magna tueri
5   per campos instructa tua sine parte pericli.
7   sed nil dulcius est, bene quam munita tenere
       edita doctrina sapientum templa serena,
       despicere unde queas alios passimque videre
10 errare atque viam palantis quaerere vitae,
       certare ingenio, contendere nobilitate,
       noctes atque dies niti praestante labore
       ad summas emergere opes rerumque potiri.
       o miseras hominum mentis, o pectora caeca!
15 qualibus in tenebris vitae quantisque periclis
       degitur hoc aevi quod cumquest! nonne videre
       nil aliud sibi naturam latrare, nisi utqui
       corpore seiunctus dolor absit, mente fruatur
       iucundo sensu cura semota metuque?

1   **suave:** Understand **est**; notice the very emphatic positioning of this word at the beginning of the first line of the book and its repetition throughout the first lines of this passage.

      Turbantibus aequora ventis is an ablative absolute.

3   **quemquamst: quemquam est.**

4   **careas:** subjunctive in indirect question introduced by **cernere**, itself governed by **suave est**. Lucretius reiterates that **voluptas** is gained not out of meanness at others' suffering but of gratitude for the evils of which one has been spared.

7   **nil: nihil.**

Dulcius est governs the infinitive **tenere**.

8   **doctrina sapientum:** refers to philosophy, and Epicureanism in particular. As Lucretius tells it, the only thing that will preserve our physical and mental safety is to practice philosophy.

11–13   **certare ... potiri:** Lucretius describes the futile labor of those who work tirelessly to acquire wealth and power. **rerumque potiri:** "to gain political power." What are some modern activities that Lucretius might also count as a waste of a lifetime?

16   **hoc aevi quod cumquest: Aevi** is partitive genitive; notice what a strong emphasis Lucretius places on the brevity of human life. If life is so short, are we spending the time wisely?

16–19   **nonne videre ... metuque:** It is clear, Lucretius claims, that it is against nature to devote one's life to wealth and power, since nature so clearly desires only to be removed from bodily pain and to enjoy the pleasure of the mind. This contrast between pleasure and pain speaks to the core belief of Epicureanism, that pleasure should be sought and pain eliminated. From this belief comes the notion that Epicureans are hedonists, in the most etymologically strict sense of the word: They seek to maximize their pleasure. (But these pleasures are not those, like power and money, that will bring you pain when you lose them—they are, rather, reliable states of tranquil and serene pleasure.)

16   **videre:** an exclamatory infinitive with the subject accusative omitted (A&G §462); the subject accusative is likely **mentes**, **pectora**, or even **homines** from line 14.

17   **nil ... latrare:** indirect statement governed by **videre**; the PERSONIFICATION (or canification) of nature with **latrare** is worth mulling over.

17   **utqui: ut**, introducing the two clauses **dolor absit** and [**natura**] **fruatur**; **mente** is locative use of the ablative: "in the mind."

20 ergo corpoream ad naturam pauca videmus
    esse opus omnino, quae demant cumque dolorem,
    delicias quoque uti multas substernere possint.
    gratius interdum neque natura ipsa requirit,
    si non aurea sunt iuvenum simulacra per aedes
25 lampadas igniferas manibus retinentia dextris,
    lumina nocturnis epulis ut suppeditentur,
    nec domus argento fulget auroque renidet
    nec citharae reboant laqueata aurataque templa,
    cum tamen inter se prostrati in gramine molli
30 propter aquae rivum sub ramis arboris altae
    non magnis opibus iucunde corpora curant,
    praesertim cum tempestas adridet et anni
    tempora conspergunt viridantis floribus herbas.
    nec calidae citius decedunt corpore febres,
35 textilibus si in picturis ostroque rubenti
    iacteris, quam si in plebeia veste cubandum est.
    quapropter quoniam nil nostro in corpore gazae
    proficiunt neque nobilitas nec gloria regni,
    quod superest, animo quoque nil prodesse putandum;
40 si non forte tuas legiones per loca campi
    fervere cum videas belli simulacra cientis,
    subsidiis magnis †epicuri† constabilitas,
    ornatas armis †itastuas† pariterque animatas,
    his tibi tum rebus timefactae religiones
45 effugiunt animo pavidae; mortisque timores
    tum vacuum pectus linquunt curaque solutum.

20   **videmus:** governs the indirect statement **pauca ... esse opus** (lines 20–21); Lucretius reiterates that only a few things are necessary to vouchsafe our happiness.

21   **quae ... cumque:** should be taken as one word, **quaecumque**.

24   **si non:** Here begins an elaborate description of the frivolous items people believe will make them happy. Notice that Lucretius uses many words about light—what sort of picture does this paint of the rich man's banquet?

29   **cum tamen:** introduces a concessive **cum**-clause (A&G §549); the following lines provide a description of the pleasantly tranquil alternative offered by Epicureanism. Contrast the sense of living with nature in this alternative as opposed to the defiance of nature in the life depicted in lines 24–28.

36   **iacteris:** The second person present passive subjunctive; the voice is not so much passive as it is akin to the Greek middle voice or the reflexive: "you throw yourself," "you fling yourself."

39   **prodesse:** an indirect statement, introduced by **putandum (est)**, understanding the subjects of the **quoniam** (line 37) clause (**gazae, nobilitas, gloria**) as its accusative subject. Lucretius develops his argument here from the physical (**in corpore**, line 37) to the psychic (**animo**, line 39). In the previous lines, he claims that merely the bare necessities provided by nature are necessary for a pleasant experience; he will now turn to the mind, claiming that no amount of wealth, breeding, or power will bring peace of mind.

40   **si non:** nisi; Lucretius proposes an improbable scenario in order to mock it.

41   **cum videas:** governs the indirect statement **legiones ... fervere**; the participles **cientis** and **constabilitas** (line 42) modify **legiones** (line 40). Don't mistake **constabilitas** for a 3rd declension abstract noun!

42–43   **subsidiis ... animatas:** These lines are corrupt—a number of editors have proposed different emendations for the daggered portions.

44   **tum:** introduces the highly unlikely conclusion to the imaginary scenario: that our fear could be driven from our mind by the sheer presence of physical armies. In short, Lucretius alleges, it is foolish to believe that the fears and superstitions inculcated by religion can be fought off by military force.

quod si ridicula haec ludibriaque esse videmus,
re veraque metus hominum curaeque sequaces
nec metuunt sonitus armorum nec fera tela
50 audacterque inter reges rerumque potentis
versantur neque fulgorem reverentur ab auro
nec clarum vestis splendorem purpureai,
quid dubitas quin omni' sit haec rationi' potestas?
omnis cum in tenebris praesertim vita laboret.
55 nam veluti pueri trepidant atque omnia caecis
in tenebris metuunt, sic nos in luce timemus
interdum, nilo quae sunt metuenda magis quam
quae pueri in tenebris pavitant finguntque futura.
hunc igitur terrorem animi tenebrasque necessest
60 non radii solis neque lucida tela diei
discutiant, sed naturae species ratioque.

47 **quod si:** introduces a condition with indicative verbs; what does it mean that Lucretius uses the indicative mood rather than the subjunctive (A&G §511)?

48–49 **metus … metuunt:** Lucretius's use of POLYPTOTON emphasizes the irony of the idea of fear being afraid.

50 **rerum … potentis:** as above at 2.13, referring to those who have political power. In response to the mistaken belief articulated above at lines 37–38 (that wealth, high birth, or political power will bring happiness), Lucretius here argues that fear revels among people with these very attributes. Notice the emphatic line-initial position of **audacter**.

52 **clarum vestis splendorem purpureai:** The genitive singular ending of **purpureai** is archaic, as at 1.112 above. Notice the elegant SYNCHYSIS (interlocking word order), which mirrors the outstanding quality of the fabric: accusative adjective – genitive noun – accusative noun – genitive adjective. Lucretius's point, of course, is that fear recognizes no such human distinction between fine and rough clothing.

53   **dubitas quin:** "you doubt that" (A&G §558a).

omni' ... rationi': The final –*s* is elided from both **omni'** and **rationi'**. **Omni'** is nominative singular, agreeing with **haec**; **potestas** is the subject complement. Although military force, wealth, and reputation may be powerless in the face of irrational fear, Lucretius promises that **ratio** can drive fear from our hearts.

55   **veluti:** a striking SIMILE that effectively employs the imagery of light and dark: While they chide children for their fear of the dark, adults are more pathetic, for they are afraid in the clear light of day.

57   **nilo:** *nihilo*, adverbial; the relative clause **quae** is the object of **timemus**.

58   **fingunt:** introduces an indirect statement, **futura (esse)**.

59   **necessest:** *necesse est*; introduces the noun clause **(ut) discutiant** (line 61). Lucretius continues making his argument through light imagery: While the light of the sun cannot dispel our fear, **ratio** can. These lines repeat 1.146–48 verbatim; Lucretius employs this technique with some frequency, mimicking the practice of oral epic poets like Homer.

61   **naturae species ratioque:** Lucretius highlights both the appearance and the underlying organization of **natura**. **Ratio**, corresponding to *logos* in Greek, is a fundamental concept of ancient philosophy. It refers not only to the human capacity to reason but also to the organizational structure that underpins the entire world and all objects in it.

HORACE

Odes 1.9; 2.16; 3.26; 4.7
Standard Level and Higher Level

— Introduction to Horace —

Quintus Horatius Flaccus lived a very eventful life, associated with the most powerful people in Rome. He came from humble beginnings, born in Venusia (in southern Italy) on December 8, 65 BCE, to a freedman father. His father wanted to ensure that Horace would receive a good education, and thus he saved a good deal of money for Horace's schooling in Rome. Horace would continue his education in Athens, where he would meet Marcus Brutus. Brutus, one of the chief assassins of Julius Caesar, was in Athens looking for support; Horace joined his army but turned out to be not an impressive soldier, as he fled the battlefield (as he tells us in *Ode* 2.7). The battle he fled was the Battle of Philippi (42 BCE), where Octavian and Mark Antony defeated Brutus and Cassius. Fortunately for Horace, Octavian was quick to pardon those who had fought against him.

Upon his return to Rome, Horace began to write poetry. His first two volumes, *Satires* and *Epodes*, caught the eye of Octavian and his followers. In particular, Octavian's chief tastemaker, Maecenas, became Horace's patron, even gifting him his beloved Sabine farm. His most famed work, the *Odes*, were next to be published, followed thereafter by the *Epistles* and *Odes* Book 4. Horace also wrote works for public performance. Because of his association with Augustus's imperial court, Horace's reputation was troubled, as some considered him a mere propagandist.

The *Odes* contain Horace's most famous lines, and some of the most famous in all Latin literature. *Ode* 1.11 contains the famous **carpe diem**, though readers of the entire ode will find that the poem is not so much about working up the gumption to accomplish epic feats as it is an old-fashioned seduction poem. *Ode* 1.37 (the "Cleopatra Ode") is a celebration of Augustus's victory over Cleopatra, and contains the famous line **nunc est bibendum**. The phrase is used nowadays to commemorate occasions suitable for toasting. We can also see in this ode why Horace was criticized for compromising his poetry with praise of Augustus.

The *Odes* are inspired by Greek lyric poetry: The meters, topics, and themes are similar to those found in Sappho, Alcaeus, and Archilochus. Like these Greek poets, in the *Odes* Horace treats love, nature, and philosophy. Horace was an Epicurean, and some poems (like 1.9, 2.16, and 4.7 below) contain Epicurean themes of savoring the moment and distancing oneself from the anxieties of political life. *Ode* 3.26 is reminiscent not only of Horace's contemporary Ovid but also of Sappho 1, wherein Sappho asks for Aphrodite's (Venus's) help in wooing a beloved.

Horace, and his *Odes* in particular, have had a long and extensive afterlife. Many generations of poets and translators have adapted his poetry for new audiences. It is illuminating and enjoyable to compare these modern versions with Horace's originals.

— Meters —

Alcaic Strophe: *Odes* 1.9, 3.26
First Archilochian: *Ode* 4.7
Sapphic Strophe: *Ode* 2.16

Introduction to Horace

House of Horace, Venosa (D.N.R./Wikimedia Commons)

Modern Venosa, built near the site of the ancient city Venusia, celebrates its legacy as the birthplace of Horace. This building, traditionally known as the Casa di Orazio Flacco (House of Horace Flaccus), serves as a museum and contains reproductions of items that might have belonged to a Roman poet.

— *Ode 1.9* —

This ode displays some of the most prominent themes in Horace: scenes of nature, the brevity and uncertainty of life, carnal pleasures. Horace also touches upon Epicurean beliefs about the mutability of fortune. As with many of Horace's poems, there is a gnomic statement, or motto, that appears midway through the poem—this statement often carries the philosophical message of the poem. In this poem, it appears in the fourth stanza: **quid sit futurum cras fuge quaerere, et / quem Fors dierum cumque dabit lucro / adpone**... *The first three stanzas focus on winter, the fourth relates the philosophical message, and the final two discuss the consequences of mortality, that is, that one should enjoy one's life while one can. The poem is addressed to one Thaliarchus, a fictitious young man.*

vides ut alta stet nive candidum
Soracte, nec iam sustineant onus
    silvae laborantes geluque
    flumina constiterint acuto?

5   dissolve frigus ligna super foco
large reponens atque benignius
    deprome quadrimum Sabina,
    o Thaliarche, merum diota.

permitte divis cetera, qui simul
10 stravere ventos aequore fervido
    deproeliantis, nec cupressi
    nec veteres agitantur orni.

quid sit futurum cras fuge quaerere et
quem Fors dierum cunque dabit lucro
15 appone nec dulcis amores
    sperne puer neque tu choreas,

2   **vides ... nive:** Notice the SYNCHYSIS (interlocking word order): **Alta** modifies **nive**. This first stanza beautifully depicts the winter scene.

Soracte: a mountain ridge north of Rome; this is the nominative form, modified by **candidum** (line 1).

7   **quadrimum:** Four-year-old wine was generally considered to be quite special in the Roman world. Stanza two shifts the scene indoors to the human activity of mitigating the cold.

8   **Thaliarche:** Horace's fictitious addressee. The name is Greek: The suffix "-archus" means "ruling in" while "Thalia" is the muse of comedy, and also a noun meaning "festivities," "good cheer." "Thaliarchus" might then mean "the life of the party."

merum: Wine was typically served mixed with water in the ancient world. Unmixed wine was then, accordingly, very strong.

9   **simul: simul ac.**

10 **stravere:** syncopated form of **straverunt**.

13 **quid sit futurum cras:** This indirect question is the direct object of **quaerere**. The addressee of this stanza is Thaliarche. This stanza moves quickly from the recognition of the limitations of mortal life to the upshot, that we should enjoy its pleasures.

14 **quem ... cunque: quemcumque**, here separated. TMESIS

Lucro appone is a fiscal METAPHOR, "to count as profit."

16 **neque tu choreas:** along with **dulcis amores** (line 15), also the object of **sperne**.

> donec virenti canities abest
> morosa. nunc et Campus et areae
> lenesque sub noctem susurri
> 20 composita repetantur hora;
>
> nunc et latentis proditor intimo
> gratus puellae risus ab angulo,
> pignusque dereptum lacertis
> aut digito male pertinaci.

17   **virenti:** ablative, modifying an ELLIPTED **te**.

18   **et Campus et areae: Campus** likely refers to the Campus Martius; **areae** are playgrounds. Both terms refer not so much to the locations themselves as to the entertainment and activities available there: the diversions of youth.

19   **lenesque . . . susurri:** This entire line is the third subject of the jussive subjunctive **repetantur** (line 20).

20   **composita . . . hora:** literally, the time at which people couple, or come together.

21   **nunc:** Notice the insistent repetition of **nunc**, here and above at line 18. What effect does the repetition have?

21–22 **latentis . . . angulo:** The word order of these two lines is heavily intertwined: **Latentis** modifies **puellae**, **intimo** modifies **angulo**, and **gratus** modifies **risus**. **Risus** stands in apposition to **proditor**: Her noises give the **puella** away.

24   **male:** not in the strictly negative sense of "badly," but perhaps either "poorly" (not resisting very well) or "playfully" (teasingly).

The Pantheon, Rome (© 2012 Shutterstock Images LLC)

Following the Battle of Actium in 31 BCE, Marcus Agrippa began a building program that included the construction of the Pantheon on land that he owned in the Campus Martius. While the Campus Martius was originally an open space used for military training, by the time of the late Republic it also held both private residences and public buildings. Many of the earliest buildings on the Campus Martius commemorated military victories.

— Ode 2.16 —

In this very Epicurean poem, Horace extols the virtues of **otium**, *and in so doing he describes the fear and anxiety that dog humanity. These cannot be remedied, nor can* **otium** *be acquired, through money, fame, or high birth. Tranquillity comes from learning to make joy in one's present circumstances and calming our anxieties about what is displeasing to us or beyond our abilities. The themes and language here are very similar to those in Lucretius 2.1–61.*

   otium divos rogat in patenti
   prensus Aegaeo, simul atra nubes
   condidit lunam neque certa fulgent
      sidera nautis;

5   otium bello furiosa Thrace,
   otium Medi pharetra decori,
   Grosphe, non gemmis neque purpura ve-
      nale neque auro.

   non enim gazae neque consularis
10 summovet lictor miseros tumultus
   mentis et curas laqueata circum
      tecta volantis.

   vivitur parvo bene, cui paternum
   splendet in mensa tenui salinum
15 nec levis somnos timor aut cupido
      sordidus aufert.

1   **otium:** This important first word announces the theme of the entire poem; it is repeated in lines 5 and 6.

2   **Aegaeo:** the Aegean Sea.

3   **condidit:** in the sense of "crowd out," "cover." As in 1.9, the first stanza establishes the setting with a memorable scene from nature.

5	**otium:** Understand **rogat** as the verb governing both this and the occurrence in the next line.
7	**Grosphe:** The addressee of the poem, Pompeius Grosphus, was a wealthy landowner; he is also mentioned in *Epistles* 1.12. The final two stanzas of the poem sketch out Grosphus's life and character; there we learn that his estate is large and plentiful, in comparison to Horace's Sabine farm.
7–8	**non gemmis ... auro:** the same assertion as above in Lucretius 2.1–61, that peace of mind cannot be bought. This ideal of peace or tranquillity, called by its Greek name *ataraxia* ("freedom from disturbance"), is the ultimate goal of Epicurean and Stoic philosophies.
9	**gazae:** The same term is used above, at Lucretius 2.37, in a similar context.
10	**summovet lictor:** a technical phrase, referring to the action of lictors when clearing a space for the consul.
11	**circum:** takes **laqueata ... texta** as its object.
13	**vivitur:** impersonal, "it is lived."
13–14	**paternum ... salinum:** Note the detail that the salt shaker is inherited, rather than purchased. Moreover, the incongruence between **splendet** and **tenui** also emphasizes the simple style of life.
15	**timor aut cupido:** The simple man has few luxuries, but his life is also devoid of fear and greed. The third and fourth stanzas describe opposing lives: one of wealth, power, and angst, the other of simplicity and tranquillity.

quid brevi fortes iaculamur aevo
multa? quid terras alio calentis
sole mutamus? patriae quis exsul
20   se quoque fugit?

scandit aeratas vitiosa navis
cura nec turmas equitum relinquit,
ocior cervis et agente nimbos
    ocior Euro.

25 laetus in praesens animus quod ultra est
oderit curare et amara lento
temperet risu; nihil est ab omni
    parte beatum.

abstulit clarum cita mors Achillem,
30 longa Tithonum minuit senectus,
et mihi forsan tibi quod negarit,
    porriget hora.

17   **fortes:** meant somewhat ironically, as **brevi . . . aevo** emphasizes human mortality and frailty.

18–19   **terras . . . sole:** Notice the SYNCHYSIS, in addition to the ENJAMBMENT that pervades the entire stanza. Why do you think so many lines are ENJAMBED in this stanza?

20   **se quoque fugit:** Be sure to scan this line for the quantity of **fugit**. This line echoes an oft-expressed sentiment in philosophy, that travel is worthless if what one seeks to flee is within oneself. Cf. Seneca, *De Tranquillitate Animi* 2.13–15 in this volume, and *Epistulae Morales* 3.28.

23   **ocior:** Note the ANAPHORA, which emphasizes the inescapable speed of **cura**.

25 **laetus in praesens animus:** According to Epicureanism, this is the ideal state of the soul; it is joyful in its present circumstances, neither anxious or desirous, nor fixated on the past or the future.

26 **oderit:** perfect subjunctive; **odi** is a defective verb—it has only a perfect system, which is translated as if a present system (A&G §205). **Oderit**, like **temperet** in the next line, is thus to be translated as a jussive, "let it despise," "let it refuse." It governs the complementary infinitive **curare**, which in turn takes the relative clause **quod ultra est** (line 25) as its object.

27–28 **nihil est ... beatum:** a famous line often quoted out of context. The sentiment, however, is retained: We should be ready to take obstacles with an easygoing attitude since nothing can be wholly perfect.

29–30 **Achillem, Tithonum:** These two mythological examples are presented as opposites: Achilles died too young, while Tithonus grew ever older but never died. Cf. *Odyssey* 11.486–91, part of Achilles's moving speech in the Underworld: In retrospect he wishes to have lived a long but unremarkable life over the glorious but short one he had.

31 **negarit:** syncopated form of **negaverit**, future perfect indicative. This stanza, a contemplation on the brevity of a good quality of life, asserts the importance of living a life of good quality in the present.

> te greges centum Siculaeque circum
> mugiunt vaccae, tibi tollit hinnitum
> 35 apta quadrigis equa, te bis Afro
>   murice tinctae
>
> vestiunt lanae: mihi parva rura et
> spiritum Graiae tenuem Camenae
> Parca non mendax dedit et malignum
> 40   spernere volgus.

33   **te:** object of the preposition **circum**. The primary position of **te** indicates the shift in scene to Grosphus's bucolic surroundings. Note also the POLYPTOTON that introduces the three clauses in this stanza: **te, tibi, te.**

37   **mihi:** The final stanza shifts back to the poet's circumstances, which are meager but sufficient.

38   **Camena:** a muse, associated with the Greek muses.

39   **non mendax:** a pun on the name of the goddess Parca, on the basis of what (little, from **parcus, -a, -um**) she has given the poet: Her name doesn't belie her character. But Horace here is not complaining about the paucity of his possessions; rather, he is content with them, in Epicurean fashion. He also implies that Grosphus, despite all his possessions, may be unhappy.

39–40   **malignum spernere volgus:** also a direct object of **dedit**; **volgus** is the archaic form for **vulgus**.

Achilles statue, Corfu (© 2009 Shutterstock Images LLC)

This statue of Achilles depicts the hero in a triumphant pose. According to the *Iliad*, he knowingly chose glory and an early death over a long and undistinguished life. This statue stands on the Greek island Corfu in the gardens of Achillion Palace.

— *Ode* 3.26 —

*This ode is very similar to the elegies of Propertius, Tibullus, Gallus, and Ovid, and their predecessor Catullus. Like those poets, Horace's narrator has experienced love, and he seeks now to retire from battle. The martial metaphor, made most famous by Ovid's **militat omnis amans** (Amores 1.9), is employed here too. The end of the ode turns to Venus and asks for a sort of revenge upon the lover who spurns the speaker.*

    vixi, puellis nuper idoneus,
    et militavi non sine gloria;
        nunc arma defunctumque bello
        barbiton hic paries habebit,

5   laevum marinae qui Veneris latus
    custodit. hic, hic ponite lucida
        funalia et vectis et arcus
        oppositis foribus minacis.

    o quae beatam diva tenes Cyprum et
10   Memphin carentem Sithonia nive,
        regina, sublimi flagello
        tange Chloën semel arrogantem.

2   **militavi:** The METAPHOR of battle for love is pervasive in both the ancient and contemporary worlds. What are some modern poems or songs that make use of this METAPHOR? Why do you think the image continues to find such purchase? Notice that in both lines 1 and 2 the verb stands in first position, placing emphasis on the actions. The tense of the verbs is emphasized by **nunc** in line 3 and the future-tense **habebit** in line 4.

    non sine gloria: LITOTES; why might Horace choose to utilize this poetic device here?

3–4	**nunc arma ... habebit:** As a soldier dedicates his weapons to a god by hanging them on the temple walls, so Horace retires from the practice of seduction by hanging up his "weapons." We might compare this to the modern idiom "to hang up one's boots." Horace makes a similar dedication to Poseidon in *Ode* 1.5.
4	**barbiton:** a borrowed Greek term. The *–on* ending is accusative singular; thus **barbiton** is modified by **defunctum**.
5	**marinae:** modifies **Veneris** and refers to her birth from the sea.
7	**vectis:** from **vectis**, the noun, not **veho**. **Et arcus** is uncertain, and several alternative readings have been proposed. Some scholars believe a bow would be an inappropriate weapon for wooing someone and have supposed it is some tool to break into houses.
9	**diva:** should be taken with **o**, "o diva."
9–10	**Cyprum ... Memphin ... Sithonia:** Venus is commonly associated with Cyprus, one of her birth sites and a chief site of worship. Memphis, in Egypt, is the site of a temple to the Mesopotamian goddess Astarte, with whom Venus/Aphrodite was roughly equivalent. Sithonia is a peninsula in northern Greece.
12	**Chloën:** the Greek accusative form. Notice that its modifier **arrogantem** is intentionally held off to the last word—it has an almost causal sense here, "because she is arrogant."
	semel can be taken with both **tange** and **arrogantem**, but it is likely to be taken more closely with **tange**, as if the poet is asking that Chloe "just once" feel the pangs of love that he himself has felt for her. The image of the whip (**flagello**, line 11) is evocative of the fearful pain that comes with infatuation or unrequited love. The poet hopes that Chloe's arrogance is humbled by an experience of hopeless ardor.

— Ode 4.7 —

*This famous ode meditates on mortality and the necessary temporality of all things. Horace begins by reflecting on nature: the changes in the seasons, the passing of years. He then turns to human mortality and the inescapability of death. The philosophical statement appears in lines 7–8 (**immortalia ne speres monet annus et almum / quae rapit hora diem**) as well as later in lines 16–18.*

    diffugere nives, redeunt iam gramina campis
        arboribus comae;
    mutat terra vices et decrescentia ripas
        flumina praetereunt;
5   Gratia cum Nymphis geminisque sororibus audet
        ducere nuda choros.
    immortalia ne speres, monet annus et almum
        quae rapit hora diem.
    frigora mitescunt Zephyris, ver proterit aestas
10   interitura, simul
    pomifer Auctumnus fruges effuderit, et mox
        bruma recurrit iners.
    damna tamen celeres reparant caelestia lunae:
        nos ubi decidimus
15   quo pius Aeneas, quo dives Tullus et Ancus,
        pulvis et umbra sumus.
    quis scit an adiciant hodiernae crastina summae
        tempora di superi?
    cuncta manus avidas fugient heredis, amico
20   quae dederis animo.

1	**diffugere:** syncopated form for **diffugerunt**.
2	**comae:** refers to their leaves and buds: an interesting PERSONIFICATION of trees. **Gramina campis** and **arboribus comae** have no conjunction between them: Why does Horace employ ASYNDETON here?
3	**vices:** here, the succession of seasons.
	ripas: governed by the **praeter-** prefix in **praetereunt** in the next line.
5	**Gratia:** usually plural, but Horace here expresses the trio as **Gratia cum ... geminis sororibus**. The Graces are Aglaia, Euphrosyne, and Thalia; they almost always appear as a trio, often in nude dance, as here. Compare the depiction of the Graces here with Botticelli's famous painting *Primavera*.
7	**immortalia ne speres:** indirect command introduced by **monet**. After three couplets celebrating the joys of spring, the poem takes a sudden turn as it reiterates the mortality and temporality of it all.
8	**hora:** The antecedent of the relative clause is embedded within it.
9–12	**frigora ... iners:** These two couplets relate the cyclical progression of the seasons, emphasizing that none persists for long, but soon yields to the next.
10	**interitura:** future active participle of **intereo**, modifying **aestas** (line 9).
	simul = simul ac.
13	**damna ... lunae:** This line provides a counterexample: In the heavens, objects appear immortal. The next lines, however, are contrastive: We who have fallen are all too mortal.
15	**Aeneas ... Tullus ... Ancus:** Aeneas is, of course, the eponymous protagonist of the *Aeneid*; Tullus Hostilius was the third king of Rome; Ancus Martius was the fourth. Reunderstand **decidit/deciderunt** from the previous line.
17–18	**quis scit ... di superi:** The point of the entire ode, simply and concisely stated.
19	**cuncta:** The perspective shifts slightly, to our death and its aftermath, particularly on earth. Note the use of the future perfect with **occideris** (line 21) and **fecerit** (line 22).

> cum semel occideris et de te splendida Minos
>   fecerit arbitria,
> non, Torquate, genus, non te facundia, non te
>   restituet pietas;
> 25 infernis neque enim tenebris Diana pudicum
>   liberat Hippolytum,
> nec Lethaea valet Theseus abrumpere caro
>   vincula Pirithoo.

21 **Minos:** the Cretan king who possessed both the famous Minotaur and the labyrinth it was kept in. After his death, Minos became one of the judges of souls in the Underworld. Vergil depicts him in this role in *Aeneid* 6.

23 **Torquate:** not the legendary Titus Manlius Torquatus, slayer of Gauls. We know Torquatus is also the addressee of Horace's *Epistle* 1.5. The ANAPHORA that repeats **non Torquate/te** across three consecutive clauses drives home the inexorability of our mortality.

25–28 **infernis ... Pirithoo:** The ode closes with mythological examples of the inescapability of death: gods and heroes who, despite their strength and divinity, could not free their loved ones from the Underworld. Diana was not able to save her chaste devotee Hippolytus, and Theseus was not able to save his comrade Perithous.

SENECA

Epistulae Morales 1, 16 (SL and HL)
Standard Level and Higher Level

— Introduction to Seneca —

Lucius Annaeus Seneca was born the middle son to the rhetorician Marcus Annaeus Seneca (Seneca the Elder) in Corduba (modern Cordoba, Spain), sometime in the first decade BCE. While he was trained for a career in politics, Seneca chose philosophy instead. He served the imperial courts of both Claudius and Nero but was banished in 41 CE under the reign of Claudius. He was recalled from exile in 49 CE by Agrippina, Nero's mother, in order to serve as a tutor for the yet-adolescent emperor. While for a number of years Seneca and his cotutor Burrus were able to steer Nero wisely, Nero eventually rejected his advisers, resulting in Seneca's retirement from public service. In 65 CE, Seneca was embroiled, perhaps undeservedly, in an assassination conspiracy against Nero; as a result he was forced by the emperor to commit suicide. Tacitus in *Annales* 15.60–64 gives an account of Seneca's death, stylized in the tradition of Socrates's death.

The circumstances of Seneca's own life, particularly his enormous wealth, often seem to be in conflict with the staidness of his Stoic philosophy. He preaches an asceticism in his philosophical output that his own life seems not to have exemplified. This incongruence has been treated variously by scholars, from accusations of hypocrisy to sympathy at the struggles of a mere human.

Stoicism, like Epicureanism, was founded in Athens in the age of Aristotle. However, in contrast to Epicurus's Garden, Zeno of Citium practiced his philosophy in the center of Athens in an area known as the Painted Stoa. The Stoa was a bustling place of business and politics, and thus unlike the Epicureans—who shunned political involvement—the Stoics sought to influence social and political movements. (We may see this in Seneca's tutorship with the emperor Nero.) Stoicism, also in contrast to Epicureanism, believed in the ever-presence of divinity: The Stoic god was present in all things. Moreover, the Stoic world was a fated one, designed by the same god—all events were fated, as were one's choices. The key to Stoic happiness, then, was to recognize one's role in that world and to play it to the best of one's ability. The harmony that comes of playing one's role well, of navigating the river of one's life smoothly, constituted happiness. Like the Epicureans, the Stoics believed that an immoderate attachment to objects caused pain—we are pained when we lose objects and people we value because we erroneously believe that they belong to us and that they will remain with us forever.

Seneca's philosophical works include various essays, written throughout his political career, and the *Epistulae Morales*, written late in life. He was also the author of nine tragedies, based on Greek originals, and a satire on the emperor Claudius. Scholars have long sought to explain the relationship between Seneca's philosophical works and his tragedies, particularly as the latter are especially emotionally tortured and grotesque. The naked violence of the tragedies is particularly shocking in light of the tranquillity espoused by Stoic philosophy.

Seneca's writing is a prime example of the Latin stylistics of the early imperial period, also known as Silver Latin. As we can see in the language of his letters, Seneca's rhetorical style is brisk and clipped, full of wordplay and rhythm. It is a stark contrast to, for example, Cicero's rhetorical style, which exemplifies periodicity and hypotaxis.

Introduction to Seneca

Seneca (I, Calidius, Wikimedia Commons)

This double herm depicts Seneca, identified by a Latin inscription, on one side and Socrates, identified by a Greek inscription, on the other. Herms (a sculpture of a head, sometimes with a torso also) originated in ancient Greece in connection with the cult of Hermes and were believed to provide protection at crossroads and boundaries. Later Roman herms often portrayed writers, philosophers, and other public figures.

— *Epistulae Morales* 1 —

In this, the opening letter to the Epistulae Morales, *Seneca describes the proper Stoic attitude toward possessions and, in particular, time. As the Stoics saw it, humans become too attached to possessions (including life itself); as a result, the loss of these possessions causes unnecessary pain. Time alone is ours, and even then, only the present: Past time is already gone, while the future is uncertain. The best we can do, Seneca says, is to spend our time wisely, as if it were money.*

[1] ita fac, mi Lucili; vindica te tibi, et tempus, quod adhuc aut auferebatur aut subripiebatur aut excidebat, collige et serva. persuade tibi hoc sic esse ut scribo: quaedam tempora eripiuntur nobis, quaedam subducuntur, quaedam effluunt.
5   turpissima tamen est iactura, quae per neglegentiam fit.

1   **Lucili:** Lucilius is the addressee of the *Epistulae Morales*. Although we have come to believe that these letters are fictitious and were never actually sent to Lucilius (nor do we have any replies from Lucilius), we believe that Lucilius was nonetheless a real historical figure. What information we do know about him is from Seneca himself: that he was born in Pompeii, that he came from a humble background, and that he had, at the time of the composition of the *Epistulae Morales*, risen to the position of procurator of Sicily. In the letters, Lucilius is depicted as Seneca's disciple, someone a few steps, philosophically, behind Seneca, whom Seneca advises, encourages, and occasionally chides. Nonetheless Seneca makes explicit that he himself is also a **proficiens** (one who is still progressing in philosophy, in contrast to the **sapiens**, the wise man who has perfected himself).

vindica te tibi: Seneca uses the METAPHOR of slavery to describe a life without philosophical awareness or purpose. While the social and political pressures of the world enslave us with their obligations and stress, philosophy provides us with a method for finding mental and spiritual freedom. Typically the verb **vindico** takes the accusative of the person freed and the dative of the person who benefits; Seneca uses two reflexives, **te** and **tibi**, to reinforce that Lucilius is to take this action upon himself, and for his own benefit.

2   **aut auferebatur aut subripiebatur aut excidebat:** Seneca was the son of a rhetorician (Seneca the Elder), and his writing is marked by the striking use of rhetoric. In this use of ANAPHORA, he repeats the conjunction **aut** in a series of three verbs. While all three verbs are in the imperfect tense (to denote repeated action) they exhibit variety in both voice (active and passive) and in prefix. Importantly, the prefixes of the verbs each demonstrate a different direction in which time is being stolen: away from us (**au-**), out from under us (**sub-**), and out of us (**ex-**). Seneca thus reiterates the seriousness of the situation: Time is slipping away from us, at every moment and in every direction.

2–3   **collige et serva:** Notice again Seneca's rhetorical structuring in this first sentence: Two pairs of imperative verbs, **fac . . . vindica** and **collige . . . serva**, surround the relative clause comprised of three verbs in the imperfect tense: **auferebatur . . . subripiebatur . . . excidebat**.

3   **serva:** The imperative, with its similarity to the noun **serva/-us**, echoes the theme of slavery from **vindica** above.

persuade tibi: Note that **persuadeo** takes the dative of the person persuaded. Here, the indirect statement **hoc sic esse ut scribo** is the object of which the person is persuaded.

3–4   **quaedam . . . quaedam . . . quaedam:** another use of ANAPHORA. This clause mirrors the relative clause above: Each clause has a verb with a different prefix, and the last verb is in the active voice.

iactura: a noun, not a verb form.

et si volueris attendere, magna pars vitae elabitur male agentibus, maxima nihil agentibus, tota vita aliud agentibus.

[2] quem mihi dabis, qui aliquod pretium tempori ponat, qui diem aestimet, qui intellegat se cotidie mori? in hoc enim fallimur, quod mortem prospicimus; magna pars eius iam praeterit. quicquid aetatis retro est, mors tenet.

fac ergo, mi Lucili, quod facere te scribis, omnes horas complectere. sic fiet, ut minus ex crastino pendeas, si hodierno manum inieceris. [3] dum differtur, vita transcurrit. omnia, Lucili, aliena sunt, tempus tantum nostrum est. in huius rei unius fugacis ac lubricae possessionem natura nos misit, ex qua expellit quicumque vult.

6   **volueris:** future perfect indicative in a future more vivid/future indicative condition. While Latin uses the future tense in these conditions, in English we tend to translate them using the present tense. For the use of the future *perfect* aspect, see A&G §516c.

7   **agentibus:** used substantively, dative of disadvantage: "from those doing . . ." Another TRICOLON, describing the costs of a life badly spent. Seneca's math is interesting: Evildoers waste a great part of their lives, do-nothings waste the greater part of their lives, but busybodies waste their entire lives. The last colon is intentionally surprising: Seneca leads us to believe that the final colon will praise the productivity of those who are active, or that he will condemn as completely lost the lives of wastrels. Instead, Seneca criticizes those very lives that society praises: those who spend their days involved in political intrigue, social gossip, and general haste. In doing so, Seneca marks sharply the distance between the philosophical life he espouses and the one conventionally esteemed, one conspicuous in fame, reputation, and influence.

8   **quem mihi dabis:** a RHETORICAL QUESTION directed at the addressee; **dabis** in the sense of "providing an example in discourse."

8–9 **qui ... qui ... qui:** another TRICOLON introduced by ANAPHORA. This TRICOLON stands in typical Ciceronian order, with the two initial cola providing the backdrop for the third; while the first two cola are simple transitive statements (the first has a direct and indirect object, the second only a direct object), the third colon uses **intellegat** to introduce an indirect statement, **se cotidie mori**. **Ponat, aestimet,** and **intellegat** are subjunctives, indicating "the sort of man who . . ." (relative clause of characteristic, A&G §535.)

The first two cola also introduce a recurrent theme in Seneca's *Epistulae Morales*, and in this letter in particular: the METAPHOR of time as money. **Pretium ... ponat** refers to the setting of prices, and **aestimet** refers to the act of appraisal. Seneca proposes that we treat our time as we do our money, but with the one exception that we can never gain more time (as one could earn money). Time is, therefore, more precious a commodity than money. Do we use the same METAPHOR today?

10–11 **prospicimus ... praeterit:** Seneca seeks to question another conventional practice, that we believe that death is before us (notice the prefix **pro-** on **prospicimus**) when it is, he claims, already upon us (**praeter-**). As he explains, whatever time we have already spent in our lives belongs to death, since we cannot recover it.

13–14 **fiet ... inieceris:** future indicative and future perfect indicative in a future more vivid/future indicative condition, as above at **volueris** (line 6).

13 **ut ... pendeas:** substantive result clause following **fiet** (A&G §568).

15 **aliena:** Seneca emphasizes that all of our possessions are, in a sense, "borrowed." This term, too, relates to the commercial METAPHOR: **Aes alienum** is the technical term for a debt. The METAPHOR continues to the end of the section with other commercial terminology: **imputari** (line 19), **debere** (line 20), **reddere** (line 22).

16–17 **huius rei unius ... qua:** refers to **tempus**.

17 **expellit:** subject is **quicumque**.

et tanta stultitia mortalium est, ut quae minima et vilissima sunt, certe reparabilia, imputari sibi, cum impetravere,
20 patiantur; nemo se iudicet quicquam debere, qui tempus accepit, cum interim hoc unum est, quod ne gratus quidem potest reddere.

[4] interrogabis fortasse, quid ego faciam, qui tibi ista praecipio. fatebor ingenue: quod apud luxuriosum sed
25 diligentem evenit, ratio mihi constat inpensae. non possum me dicere nihil perdere, sed quid perdam et quare et quemadmodum, dicam; causas paupertatis meae reddam, sed evenit mihi, quod plerisque non suo vitio ad inopiam redactis: omnes ignoscunt, nemo succurrit.

30 [5] quid ergo est? non puto pauperem, cui quantulumcumque superest, sat est. tu tamen malo serves tua, et bono tempore incipies. nam ut visum est maioribus nostris, sera parsimonia in fundo est. non enim tantum minimum in imo, sed pessimum remanet. vale.

18–20   **ut ... patiantur:** result clause following **tanta**; the subject of **patiantur** is **mortales**, implied by **mortalium**. The structure of this result clause is somewhat convoluted: The subjunctive verb **patiantur** introduces the indirect statement **quae ... imputari sibi**, with the relative clause **quae ... sunt** as the subject of the indirect statement. The **cum**-clause is inserted as an aside within the result clause.

19   **impetravere:** syncopated form of **impetraverunt**.

20   **iudicet:** jussive subjunctive, introduces the indirect statement **se ... debere**.

20–22   **debere ... gratus ... reddere:** a slight (but intentional) paradox, that we are not to consider the acquisition of something we cannot repay to be a debt.

23 **faciam:** subjunctive in indirect question.

24 **praecipio:** in the sense of "to lay out precepts" or "to prescribe."

25 **ratio ... inpensae:** The commercial METAPHOR continues: Seneca's bank-account tallies.

29 **omnes ... nemo:** an example of Seneca's rhetorical style: two short clauses in parallel construction, with complementary meanings but opposing subjects.

30–31 **quantulumcumque superest:** The relative clause is the subject of the larger relative clause in which it is embedded, **cui ... sat est**. The JUXTAPOSITION of **superest** and **sat est** is another moment of Senecan style: The words appear similar but seem initially to express a paradox. Notice also that Seneca uses the DIMINUTIVE **quantulumcumque**.

31 **serves:** subjunctive after **malo**; but **incipies** is future indicative.

32 **sera parsimonia in fundo est:** To understand the sense of this idiom, imagine—as I think Seneca here does—a jug of wine: If we are too late in our frugality, the jug will already be run down to the bottom. And, as Seneca next points out, only dregs remain at the bottom of a wine jug.

— *Epistulae Morales 16* —

In this letter, Seneca emphasizes the value of a philosophical lifestyle: While life is frequently unpredictable and challenging, philosophy offers the best therapy for the vicissitudes of fortune. Regardless of one's belief in divinity, fate, or pure chance, a good habituation toward philosophical thinking, Seneca says, will grant us inner peace when we meet with obstacles. Part of proper philosophical habituation, Seneca explains, is knowing the difference between real and false desires. Becoming aware of this distinction will prevent us from falling into a never-ending cycle of want that will only frustrate and disappoint us in the end.

[1] liquere hoc tibi, Lucili, scio, neminem posse beate vivere, ne tolerabiliter quidem sine sapientiae studio, et beatam vitam perfecta sapientia effici, ceterum tolerabilem etiam inchoata. sed hoc, quod liquet, firmandum et altius cotidiana meditatione figendum est; plus operis est in eo, ut proposita custodias quam ut honesta proponas. perseverandum est et assiduo studio robur addendum, donec bona mens sit quod bona voluntas est.

[2] itaque tibi apud me pluribus verbis aut affirmatione iam nil opus; intellego multum te profecisse. quae scribis, unde veniant, scio; non sunt ficta nec colorata.

1   **liquere hoc tibi:** indirect statement governed by **scio**.

2–4   **neminem . . . studio . . . beatam . . . inchoata:** two indirect statements that explain the content of **hoc**. Notice the repetition of **beate** in **beatam** and **tolerabiliter** in **tolerabilem**: The second clause expounds on the first by specifying the degree of wisdom required for these lives.

3–4   **tolerabilem . . . inchoata:** Understand **vitam** and **sapientia** from the previous clause.

4–5   **cotidiana meditatione:** Seneca encourages the practice of daily meditation: At the end of every day, we should reflect on our day and ask ourselves whether we are satisfied with our day.

5–6 **plus ... proponas:** Seneca displays keen insight into human behavior; anyone who has made a New Year's resolution can attest that keeping the resolution is far harder than making it. Notice, again, Seneca's fondness for repeating the same word roots but in different parts of speech (POLYPTOTON).

7 **donec:** for use with subjunctive, see A&G §556a, note.

7–8 **quod bona voluntas est:** This relative clause is the predicate of the previous clause, **bona mens sit**. The contrast of **voluntas** and **mens** (and the attendant contrast of **sit** and **est**) succinctly reiterates the importance of habituation (**assiduo studio**) in turning desire into actual reality.

10 **opus:** Understand **est**; takes the dative of the person who needs and the ablative of what is needed. **Nil** is adverbial: "not any need," "no need."

profecisse: Seneca uses a verb that echoes the term used for adherents of Stoicism (**proficiens**). Throughout the *Epistulae Morales*, Seneca gives the impression that his purported interlocutor, Lucilius, is making progress in his practice of Stoicism. This progress is, of course, fictitious, but it is worth considering why Seneca would build such a "plotline" into this series of letters.

10–11 **scribis ... veniant:** Notice Seneca's use of *VARIATIO*: The first clause is a relative clause (with an indicative verb), while the second is an indirect statement (with a subjunctive verb). Both clauses are governed by the main verb **scio**. Once again, Seneca's reference to a letter from Lucilius (**quae scribis**) lends the letter a sense of reality or authenticity.

dicam tamen quid sentiam: iam de te spem habeo, nondum
fiduciam. tu quoque idem facias volo; non est, quod tibi
cito et facile credas. excute te et varie scrutare et observa;
15 illud ante omnia vide, utrum in philosophia an in ipsa vita
profeceris. [3] non est philosophia populare artificium nec
ostentationi paratum. non in verbis, sed in rebus est. nec in
hoc adhibetur, ut cum aliqua oblectatione consumatur
dies, ut dematur otio nausia. animum format et fabricat,
20 vitam disponit, actiones regit, agenda et omittenda
demonstrat, sedet ad gubernaculum et per ancipitia
fluctuantium derigit cursum. sine hac nemo intrepide potest
vivere, nemo secure. innumerabilia accidunt singulis horis,
quae consilium exigant, quod ab hac petendum est. [4]
25 dicet aliquis: "quid mihi prodest philosophia, si fatum
est? quid prodest, si deus rector est? quid prodest, si casus
imperat? nam et mutari certa non possunt et nihil praeparari
potest adversus incerta; sed aut consilium meum occupavit
deus decrevitque quid facerem, aut consilio meo nihil fortuna
30 permittit."

12–13   **spem ... fiduciam:** Seneca once again contrasts future potential
with current reality; Lucilius shows promise, if he is persistent in his
habits, of becoming secure in his practice—but he is not there yet.

13   **facias:** a subjunctive noun clause (understand **ut**) instead of the
more common infinitive after **volo**.

14   **credas:** present subjunctive in a relative clause of characteristic.
Credo takes the dative of the person believed.

excute te: a wonderfully physical and visceral image; Seneca's graphic imagery, particularly regarding the body, is observable both in his
philosophical prose works and in his tragedies (the latter of which
inspired Elizabethan tragedians like Shakespeare).

scrutare: imperative form of the deponent verb **scrutor**.

15 **utrum in philosophia an in ipsa vita:** Seneca anticipates a simplistic response from Lucilius; thus he pushes the question with this disjuncture: Have you really made progress, or have you merely expended time? Seneca refuses to let Lucilius off easy; elsewhere he describes a true friend as one who discourages one from vices.

18–19 **consumatur ... dematur:** present subjunctives in purpose clauses; **otio** is likely here an ablative of separation (though **dematur** also takes the dative). Notice that all three verbs in this sentence are in the passive voice, in contrast to the series of present active indicative verbs in the next sentence.

21–22 **gubernaculum ... derigit cursum:** Seneca is fond of the nautical METAPHOR for the governance of one's life. In Book 6 of the *Epistulae Morales*, he writes of a sailing trip he took to Baiae and of falling victim to seasickness—we may consider the ramifications of this supposed trip in light of the nautical METAPHOR.

25 **quid mihi prodest philosophia:** These are common objections raised against Stoicism, since the fatedness of all events is one of its tenets. Seneca widens the objection here to include nonfated philosophies, however: Regardless of whether events are governed by fate, divinity, or sheer chance, what good is philosophy, if we cannot change the course of events? Seneca's answer is very Stoic: Philosophy is therapeutic.

[5] quidquid est ex his, Lucili, vel si omnia haec sunt, philosophandum est: sive nos inexorabili lege fata constringunt, sive arbiter deus universi cuncta disposuit, sive casus res humanas sine ordine impellit et iactat, philosophia nos tueri debet. haec adhortabitur, ut deo libenter pareamus, ut fortunae contumaciter; haec docebit, ut deum sequaris, feras casum. [6] sed non est nunc in hanc disputationem transeundum, quid sit iuris nostri, si providentia in imperio est, aut si fatorum series inligatos trahit, aut si repentina ac subita dominantur; illo nunc revertor, ut te moneam et exhorter, ne patiaris impetum animi tui delabi et refrigescere. contine illum et constitue, ut habitus animi fiat, quod est impetus.

[7] iam ab initio, si te bene novi, circumspicies, quid haec epistula munusculi attulerit. excute illam, et invenies. non est quod mireris animum meum; adhuc de alieno liberalis sum. quare autem alienum dixi? quicquid bene dictum est ab ullo, meum est. istuc quoque ab Epicuro dictum est: "si ad naturam vives, numquam eris pauper; si ad opiniones, numquam eris dives." [8] exiguum natura desiderat, opinio immensum. congeratur in te quicquid multi locupletes possederant. ultra privatum pecuniae modum fortuna te provehat, auro tegat, purpura vestiat, eo deliciarum opumque perducat, ut terram marmoribus abscondas, non tantum habere tibi liceat, sed calcare divitias. accedant statuae et picturae et quicquid ars ulla luxuriae elaboravit; maiora cupere ab his disces.

39	**inligatos:** Understand **nos**.
42	**delabi et refrigescere:** Notice the strong imagery evoked by the very physical word choice.
43	**habitus ... impetus:** As above, Seneca reiterates the importance of habituation in ethical practice.
44–45	**quid ... munusculi:** Many of Seneca's letters close with a quotation from a philosopher (very frequently Epicurus). He refers to these as his "gifts" to Lucilius.
46	**mireris:** subjunctive in a relative clause of characteristic.
47–48	**quicquid bene ... meum est:** a famous sentence, often quoted out of context. Here, Seneca means merely that he is free to quote a line from another author, if it is apt.
51	**congeratur:** the first in a series of jussive subjunctives; Seneca outlines an imaginary situation of incredible wealth.
52	**privatum:** "appropriate for an individual citizen."
53	**eo:** Understand **loco**.
	opum: from **ops**; take care not to confuse with **opus** and **opera**.
54	**ut ... abscondas:** result clause.
54–55	**non tantum ... sed:** These structuring principles ("not only ... but [also]") emphasize the outrageous behavior resulting from extravagant wealth described in **calcare divitias**.
56	**luxuriae:** dative.
56–57	**maiora ... disces:** After engrossing his reader in a detailed description of outrageous wealth, Seneca dispels any pleasure we may have experienced with a brief and incisive conclusion: Plenty begets desire.

[9] naturalia desideria finita sunt; ex falsa opinione nascentia ubi desinant, non habent. nullus enim terminus falso est.
60 viam eunti aliquid extremum est; error immensus est. retrahe ergo te a vanis, et cum voles scire, quod petes, utrum naturalem habeat an caecam cupiditatem, considera, num possit alicubi consistere. si longe progresso semper aliquid longius restat, scito id naturale non esse. vale.

58 **naturalia . . . opinione:** Seneca reiterates the distinction between living for nature and living for reputation: Natural desires (for the necessities of life) may be satisfied, while desires aimed at acquiring a good reputation will always multiply. We may easily apply this to our own lives today: What are the very basic necessities that we need to live? What are other things or situations we desire in order to maintain our standing among our friends, elders, and even strangers? According to Seneca, these latter desires can never be satisfied; they only teach us to want more things.

nascentia: Understand **desideria** from the previous clause.

59 **desinant:** present subjunctive in the indirect question (**ubi desinant**), which is the direct object of **habent**.

60 **error immensus est:** Don't be led astray by English derivatives! Seneca is using the image of a traveler to illustrate his argument: One traveler follows the road, while the other wanders aimlessly. Only one reaches the destination.

62–63 **num possit alicubi consistere:** Seneca provides us with a litmus test for distinguishing natural from reputation-driven desires. Try evaluating some of your desires according to his test—do you agree with his criterion?

63 **longe progresso:** ablative absolute; understand **te**. This clause revisits the image of the wandering traveler.

64 **scito:** future imperative.

SENECA

De Tranquillitate Animi 2–3
Higher Level Only

— Introduction to *De Tranquillitate Animi* —

Information on the life and works of Seneca may be found in the introduction to Seneca on page 115.

— *De Tranquillitate Animi* 2.1–2.9 —

Among Seneca's philosophical output, in addition to the Epistulae Morales, are a number of longer philosophical pieces. As a group they are often called "essays" or "dialogues." While they are not dialogues in the more traditional Platonic sense (Plato's dialogues feature Socrates conversing with others), Seneca's dialogues are not strict academic essays insofar as they feature an interlocutor or an explicit addressee. This dialogue is addressed to, and features the voice of (in Section 1, which is not part of your selection), one Serenus. While we know that Serenus, like Lucilius, was a real individual, the choice of him as an addressee is intentional: This Serenus suffers from a lack of serenity. Ironically, he is unable to acquire tranquillity because he works himself up over his inability to be tranquil. Seneca will advise him to be patient with himself.

[1] Quaero mehercules iam dudum, Serene, ipse tacitus, cui talem adfectum animi similem putem, nec ulli propius admoverim exemplo quam eorum, qui ex longa et gravi valitudine expliciti motiunculis levibusque interim offensis
5   perstringuntur et cum reliquias effugerunt, suspicionibus tamen inquietantur medicisque iam sani manum porrigunt et omnem calorem corporis sui calumniantur. horum, Serene, non parum sanum est corpus, sed sanitati parum adsuevit: sicut est quidam tremor etiam tranquilli maris, utique [lacus,]
10 cum ex tempestate requievit.

[2] opus est itaque non illis durioribus, quae etiam transcucurrimus, ut alicubi obstes tibi, alicubi irascaris, alicubi instes gravis: sed illud, quod ultimum venit, ut fidem tibi habeas et recta ire te via credas, nihil avocatus transversis
15 multorum vestigiis passim discurrentium, quorumdam circa ipsam errantium viam.

[3] quod desideras autem, magnum et summum est deoque vicinum, non concuti. hanc stabilem animi sedem Graeci

εὐθυμίαν vocant, de qua Democriti volumen egregium est.
20 ego tranquillitatem voco.

1   **Quaero:** Latin has no perfect progressive form but rather expresses an ongoing action that began in the past with a present tense and **iam dudum**.

2   **putem:** present subjunctive in indirect question.

3   **admoverim:** perfect subjunctive expressing potential.

4   **valitudine:** refers here to bad health rather than good health. Seneca employs the medical METAPHOR, which analogizes physical health to the health of the soul—this is a common METAPHOR throughout Seneca's works and in philosophical literature in general.

7   **horum:** refers to the people who were recently ill.

8   **parum sanum . . . sanitati parum:** a typically Senecan construction; he employs virtually identical words in two clauses in CHIASTIC order, but the clauses express opposing ideas.

9   **tremor:** This image nicely encapsulates Seneca's description of the recently ill.

12 **transcucurrimus:** perfect indicative.

14 **nihil:** adverbial, "not at all."

15 **quorumdam:** from **quidam**.

18 **concuti:** passive infinitive. Seneca stresses to Serenus that what Serenus seeks is absolute perfection in his philosophical practices. Like the recently ill, Serenus needs to have confidence in his progress toward good philosophical health, rather than overanalyzing all of his symptoms.

19 **εὐθυμίαν:** from the Greek *eu* ("good") and *thumos* ("spirit," "heart"), and commonly translated as "contentment."

nec enim imitari et transferre verba ad illorum formam necesse est: res ipsa, de qua agitur, aliquo signanda nomine est, quod adpellationis Graecae vim debet habere, non faciem.

[4] ergo quaerimus, quomodo animus semper aequalis secundoque cursu eat propitiusque sibi sit et sua laetus adspiciat et hoc gaudium non interrumpat, sed placido statu maneat nec adtollens se umquam nec deprimens: id tranquillitas erit. quomodo ad hanc perveniri possit, in universum quaeramus: sumes tu ex publico remedio quantum voles.

[5] totum interim vitium in medium protrahendum est, ex quo agnoscet quisque partem suam. simul tu intelleges, quanto minus negotii habeas cum fastidio tui quam hi, quos ad professionem speciosam adligatos et sub ingenti titulo laborantis in sua simulatione pudor magis quam voluntas tenet.

[6] omnes in eadem causa sunt, et hi qui levitate vexantur ac taedio adsiduaque mutatione propositi, quibus semper magis placet quod reliquerunt, et illi, qui marcent et oscitantur. adice eos, qui non aliter quam quibus difficilis somnus est, versant se et hoc atque illo modo componunt, donec quietem lassitudine inveniant: statum vitae suae formando subinde in eo novissime manent, in quo illos non mutandi odium, sed senectus ad novandum pigra deprendit.

adice et illos, qui non inconstantiae vitio parum leves sunt, sed inertiae, et vivunt non quomodo volunt, sed quomodo coeperunt.

21   **transferre verba:** Translating Greek philosophical terms into Latin was a fraught topic among Roman philosophers. Ought the term be translated literally from Greek into Latin, as Cicero did when he invented the word **qualitas** to translate the Greek *poiotēs*? (Both terms are the abstract noun forms of the interrogative adjective "of what sort?") Seneca here disagrees with that guideline, preferring to emphasize the force (**vim**) of the word over the form (**faciem**).

28–29   **in universum:** a phrase, "in general."

29   **quaeramus:** jussive subjunctive.

       ex publico remedio: Seneca proposes that he and Serenus come to a general understanding of tranquillity, from which Serenus can select what bits of advice are most useful for him.

33   **quanto:** ablative of degree of difference, "how much less"; **negotii** is partitive genitive with **minus**.

       tui: objective genitive: "disgust at yourself."

33–36   **hi ... tenet:** a resounding condemnation of those who are busy without good self-reflection as to how they spend their time, and why they value these activities.

39   **quod reliquerunt:** This relative clause is the subject of **placet**.

[7] innumerabiles deinceps proprietates sunt, sed unus effectus vitii, sibi displicere. hoc oritur ab intemperie animi et cupiditatibus timidis aut parum prosperis: ubi aut non audent, quantum concupiscunt, aut non consequuntur et in spem toti prominent, semper instabiles mobilesque sunt, quod necesse est accidere pendentibus ad vota sua. omni via pergunt et inhonesta se ac difficilia docent coguntque, et ubi sine praemio labor est, torquet illos inritum dedecus, nec dolent prava se, [sed] frustra voluisse.

[8] tunc illos et poenitentia coepti tenet et incipiendi timor subrepitque illa animi iactatio non invenientis exitum, quia nec imperare cupiditatibus suis nec obsequi possunt, et cunctatio vitae parum se explicantis et inter destituta vota torpentis animi situs.

[9] quae omnia graviora sunt, ubi odio infelicitatis operosae ad otium perfugerunt et ad secreta studia, quae pati non potest animus ad civilia erectus agendique cupidus et natura inquies, parum scilicet in se solatiorum habens: ideo detractis oblectationibus, quas ipsae occupationes discurrentibus praebent, domum, solitudinem, parietes non fert, invitus adspicit se sibi relictum.

48–49 **unus effectus:** Seneca observes that, despite the many causes and types of people affected, the end result is the same: a lack of tranquillity.

53 **ad vota sua:** Seneca finds that desires are the origin of unhappiness—how so? How does wanting lead to unhappiness?

56 **frustra voluisse:** indirect statement serves as the direct object of **dolent**; understand **se**.

58 **invenientis:** genitive, modifying **animi**.

59 **imperare cupiditatibus suis nec obsequi:** Notice Seneca's skill in selecting two verbs that not only both take the dative **cupiditatibus** but have complementary meanings and voices (active and deponent).

61 **situs:** here, the noun.

64 **animus ad civilia erectus:** Seneca speaks specifically of the temperament suited to political activity—these individuals can find no peace in leisure. Serenus, it seems, might be of this ilk; later on (in Section 4) Seneca recommends to Serenus that he participate in political life in whatever way he is most useful. This position is in stark contrast to another philosophical school, the Epicureans, who espoused the view that their adherents remove themselves from political life altogether because it was corrupting and fruitless.

66 **discurrentibus:** refers to the people who need constant stimulation. Seneca once again makes a keen observation about human psychology: Isn't this insight true also of our contemporary world? What are our modern **oblectationes**?

— *De Tranquillitate Animi* 2.10–2.15 —

In this section, Seneca discusses the restlessness of those without a settled mind and argues that an external change of scenery can do nothing to dispel inner turmoil. He describes the futile travels of those who always seek new locales but cannot escape themselves.

[10] hinc illud est taedium et displicentia sui et nusquam residentis animi volutatio et otii sui tristis atque aegra patientia, utique ubi causas fateri pudet et tormenta introrsus egit verecundia, in angusto[que] inclusae cupiditates sine exitu se ipsae strangulant: inde moeror marcorque et mille fluctus mentis incertae, quam spes inchoatae habent suspensam, deploratam, tristem. inde ille adfectus otium suum detestantium querentiumque nihil ipsos habere quod agant, et alienis incrementis inimicissima invidia. alit enim livorem infelix inertia et omnes destrui cupiunt, quia se non potuere provehere.

[11] ex hac deinde aversatione alienorum processuum et suorum desperatione obirascens fortunae animus et de saeculo querens et in angulos se retrahens et poenae incubans suae, dum illum taedet sui pigetque. natura enim humanus animus agilis est et pronus ad motus. grata omnis illi excitandi se abstrahendique materia est, gratior pessimis quibusque ingeniis, quae occupationibus libenter deteruntur, ut ulcera quaedam nocituras manus adpetunt et tactu gaudent et foedam corporum scabiem delectat, quicquid exasperat: non aliter dixerim his mentibus, in quas cupiditates velut mala ulcera eruperunt, voluptati esse laborem vexationemque.

1	**nusquam:** modifies **residentis**. There are four subjects of this sentence: **taedium, displicentia, volutatio,** and **patientia**. Notice how each of the noun clauses expressing each of the subjects grows progressively longer as the sentence proceeds.
4	**in angusto[que] inclusae cupiditates:** an interesting image, as Seneca likens **cupiditates** to living creatures trapped in a cage.
6–7	**spes inchoatae ... deploratam:** Notice the tight parallelism between the two clauses that express two stages of wishing: at the beginning, when one still holds out hope, and later, when hopes have been dashed. Seneca does not address the fulfillment of desires: He is focused here on the negative effects of unfulfilled wishes.
8	**detestantium querentiumque:** present active participles, genitive plural; these refer, again, to the people who have abandoned politics because they failed to achieve their desires. **Querentium** introduces an indirect statement (**nihil ipsos habere**), which in turn takes as its direct object a relative clause (**quod agant**).
11	**potuere:** syncopated form of **potuerunt**.
12–13	**aversatione ... desperatione:** Seneca uses CHIASTIC word order to hold both objects of **ex** together.
13–14	**obirascens ... querens ... retrahens ... incubans:** four parallel participial clauses describing the grieving process of the **animus**.
19	**ut ulcera:** a graphic image from Seneca: Desires "break out" on minds like sores on skin; and just as some sores yearn to be touched and scratched, similarly any stimulation is felt to be pleasurable to the mind captivated by desire.
21	**dixerim:** potential subjunctive.

[12] sunt enim quaedam, quae corpus quoque nostrum cum quodam dolore delectent, ut versare se et mutare nondum fessum latus, et alio atque alio positu ventilari. qualis ille Homericus Achilles est, modo pronus, modo supinus, in varios habitus se ipse conponens, quod proprium aegri est, nihil diu pati et mutationibus ut remediis uti.

[13] inde peregrinationes suscipiuntur vagae et litora pererrantur et modo mari se, modo terra experitur semper praesentibus infesta levitas. nunc Campaniam petamus. iam delicata fastidio sunt. inculta videantur: Bruttios et Lucaniae saltus persequamur. aliquid tamen inter deserta amoeni requiratur, in quo luxuriosi oculi longo locorum horrentium squalore releventur: Tarentum petatur laudatusque portus et hiberna coeli mitioris regio vel antiquae satis opulenta turbae. iam flectamus cursum ad urbem. nimis diu a plausu et fragore aures vacaverunt. iuvat iam et humano sanguine frui.

24 **ut:** "such as"; with infinitives that define the content of **quaedam**: **versare, mutare, ventilari**.

26 **Homericus Achilles:** Book 24 of the *Iliad* opens with Achilles unable to sleep, tossing and turning with grief for his dead comrade Patroclus.

27 **habitus:** from **habitus, habitūs, m.** (4th declension noun), not a verb form.

31 **petamus:** jussive subjunctive. Campania was a region around the Bay of Naples, an area known for opulence and excess. While it was a popular vacation area, it also had a reputation for dissolute behavior—one might compare it to modern-day cities like Las Vegas, Dubai, or Macau.

32 **fastidio:** dative of purpose (A&G §382).

32–33 **Bruttios et Lucaniae saltus:** regions just south of Campania, extending from Paestum to the boot tip of Italy. In contrast to Campania, however, these regions were rugged, mountainous, and sparsely inhabited.

33 **amoeni:** partitive genitive with **aliquid** (A&G §346.3).

35 **releventur:** subjunctive in a relative clause of characteristic.

Tarentum: a city in Apulia, on the boot heel of Italy; an old city, first established by the Spartans, Tarentum had a rich cultural history as part of the Greek settlement **Magna Graecia**.

37 **urbem:** Rome; we can thus trace the wanderings of these restless folk from Rome, south to Campania, then further south to Lucania, east to Tarentum, and finally back home. Seneca reiterates that for all their travels, these people are still dissatisfied and end up back where they started.

37–38 **plausu... fragore... humano sanguine:** likely refers to gladiatorial games, which Seneca elsewhere (*Epistulae Morales* 1.7) rebukes for their detrimental effect on one's character. As Seneca states in the next line, all of the sightseeing while traveling is not so different from watching gladiatorial combat: All are diversions craved by a mind without tranquillity.

[14] aliud ex alio iter suscipitur et spectacula spectaculis
40 mutantur. ut ait Lucretius:
  Hoc se quisque modo semper fugit.

sed quid prodest, si non effugit? sequitur se ipse et urget
gravissimus comes. [15] itaque scire debemus non locorum
vitium esse quo laboramus, sed nostrum: infirmi sumus
45 ad omne tolerandum, nec laboris patientes nec voluptatis,
nec nostrae nec ullius rei diutius. hoc quosdam egit ad
mortem, quod proposita saepe mutando in eadem
revolvebantur et non reliquerant novitati locum. fastidio
esse illis coepit vita et ipse mundus, et subit illud rabidarum
50 deliciarum: quousque eadem?

40   **Lucretius:** The quotation is from *DRN* 3.1068.

43–44 **non locorum vitium esse:** Seneca reiterates that discontentment does not arise from external situations but lies within oneself.

46   **quosdam:** from **quidam**.

47   **quod:** The entire statement defines **hoc**: "that…"; **proposita** is here the noun, "purpose," "intention."

48–49 **fastidio esse illis: Fastidio** is, as above (line 32), a dative of purpose; **illis** is a dative of possession ("for them"). This combination is often referred to as a *double dative* construction (A&G §382.1 note 1).

50   **quousque eadem:** Without tranquillity of mind, everything blends together—it might as well all be the same thing.

Gladiators mosaic (© 2008 Shutterstock Images LLC)

Gladiator games were a popular form of entertainment during the Roman Empire. Wealthy Romans, especially those engaged in politics, often sponsored gladiatorial combats and other games to curry favor with the populace. This mosaic, from a house in Cyprus, gives the Greek names of the gladiators: Margareites and Hellenikos.

— *De Tranquillitate Animi* 3.1–3.8 —

In this section, Seneca relates the position(s) of a fellow Stoic, Athenodorus. While at first Athenodorus seems to believe that political life is compatible with Stoic beliefs, he later reverses his position and advocates for removing oneself from politics for the sake of one's inner peace.

[1] adversus hoc taedium quo auxilio putem utendum quaeris. "Optimum erat," ut ait Athenodorus, "actione rerum et reipublicae tractatione et officiis civilibus se detinere. nam ut quidam sole atque exercitatione et cura corporis diem
5 ducunt athletisque longe utilissimum est lacertos suos roburque, cui se uni dicaverunt, maiore temporis parte nutrire: ita vobis animum ad rerum civilium certamen parantibus in opere esse [non] longe pulcherrimum est. nam cum utilem se efficere civibus mortalibusque propositum
10 habeat, simul et exercetur et proficit, qui in mediis se officiis posuit communia privataque pro facultate administrans.

[2] sed quia in hac," inquit, "tam insana hominum ambitione tot calumniatoribus in deterius recta torquentibus parum tuta simplicitas est et plus futurum semper est, quod obstet
15 quam quod succedat, a foro quidem et publico recedendum est, sed habet, ubi se etiam in privato laxe explicet magnus animus. nec ut leonum animaliumque impetus caveis coercetur, sic hominum, quorum maximae in seducto actiones sunt.

20 [3] ita tamen delituerit, ut ubicumque otium suum absconderit, prodesse velit singulis universisque ingenio, voce, consilio. nec enim is solus reipublicae prodest, qui candidatos extrahit et tuetur reos et de pace belloque

censet, sed qui iuventutem exhortatur, qui in tanta bonorum
25 praeceptorum inopia virtutem instillat animis, qui ad
pecuniam luxuriamque cursu ruentis prensat ac retrahit et, si
nihil aliud, certe moratur, in privato publicum negotium agit.

1 **quo auxilio:** ablative object of **utendum**, which takes the ablative. **Sit** is ELLIPTED from the indirect question **quo auxilio putem utendum [sit]**, which is governed by **quaeris**.

2 **Athenodorus:** a Stoic philosopher of the Augustan age, slightly before Seneca's time. None of his own work survives; we know of him through the texts of others.

10 **habeat:** subjunctive in causal **cum**-clause (A&G §549).

in mediis se officiis: The word order mimics the content of the sentence, as **se** stands in the midst of the prepositional phrase.

14 **futurum ... est:** periphrasis for **erit**.

15–16 **recedendum est:** Athenodorus reverses his position in light of the overwhelming negative aspects of engaging in political activity. Compare Athenodorus's position here with Lucretius's in *DRN* 2.7–16.

22 **nec enim is solus ... :** This elaborately structured sentence expresses the sorts of beneficial political activity that could be done in private. The sentence begins with a brisk TRICOLON describing what one typically considers to be political activity. The second half of the sentence, which describes private political activities, is more extensive: Each element of the TRICOLON (**qui ... exhortatur; qui ... instillat; qui ... prensat ac retrahit et ... certe moratur**) is more developed than the TRICOLON found in the first half. Moreover, as the TRICOLON crescendos, the third element contains not one but three verbs. The space expended on a thought seems thus to be directly reflective of the importance of the content it transmits.

[4] an ille plus praestat, qui inter peregrinos et cives aut urbanus praetor adeuntibus adsessoris verba pronuntiat, quam qui quid sit iustitia, quid pietas, quid patientia, quid fortitudo, quid mortis contemptus, quid deorum intellectus, quantumque adiutorium hominum sit bona conscientia?

[5] ergo si tempus in studia conferas, quod subduxeris officiis, non deserueris nec munus detrectaveris. neque enim ille solus militat, qui in acie stat et cornu dextrum laevumque defendit, sed qui portas tuetur et statione minus periculosa, non otiosa tamen fungitur vigiliasque servat et armamentario praeest: quae ministeria quamvis incruenta sint, in numerum stipendiorum veniunt.

[6] si te ad studia revocaveris, omne vitae fastidium effugeris nec noctem fieri optabis taedio lucis, nec tibi gravis eris nec aliis supervacuus. multos in amicitiam adtrahes adfluetque ad te optimus quisque. numquam enim, quamvis obscura virtus latet, sed mittit sui signa: quisquis dignus fuerit, vestigiis illam colliget.

[7] nam si omnem conversationem tollimus et generi humano renuntiamus vivimusque in nos tantum conversi, sequetur hanc solitudinem omni studio carentem inopia rerum agendarum: incipiemus aedificia alia ponere, alia subvertere et mare submovere et aquas contra difficultatem locorum educere et male dispensare tempus, quod nobis natura consumendum dedit:

[8] alii parce illo utimur, alii prodige. alii sic inpendimus, ut possimus rationem reddere, alii, ut nullas habeamus reliquias,
55 qua re nihil turpius est. saepe grandis natu senex nullum aliud habet argumentum, quo se probet diu vixisse, praeter aetatem."

30   **qui quid sit iustitia, quid pietas, quid patientia . . . :** Reunderstand **nuntiat** with these indirect questions. The work described is, of course, that of the philosopher. Athenodorus here makes a case that the philosopher, by inquiring into the fundamental questions that underpin political structures, does work that is as valuable as that of a political official.

34-35   **ille solus militat:** Athenodorus uses an example of another civic duty that can be performed by more public or private means. Do you agree with his claim? This question is still debated in the modern world: Some draw distinctions between combat and noncombat roles, and servicemembers and the citizenry at home.

44   **fuerit:** future perfect indicative, here.

46   **si omnem conversationem tollimus . . . :** Athenodorus stresses the importance of remaining engaged in the human community.

54   **rationem reddere:** a return to the theme of *Epistulae Morales* 1.1, wherein Seneca exhorts us to regard time as precious as money.

56   **praeter aetatem:** Athenodorus refers not to material possessions but to the necessity of making something of one's life.

This passage ends with Athenodorus's quotation. In the section immediately following, however, Seneca disagrees with Athenodorus. While Athenodorus believes that we should retire from public service to preserve our own tranquillity, Seneca recommends more thought and caution when withdrawing.

Appendix 1: Historical Timeline

Date	Historical and Political Events	Significant texts/ literary events
BCE		
341		Birth of Epicurus
270		Death of Epicurus
c. 100		Birth of Lucretius
65		Birth of Horace
c. 50–40		Death of Lucretius
49	Caesar crosses the Rubicon	
44	Caesar assassinated	
23–11		Publication of Horace's *Odes*
9	Death of Drusus the Elder (father of Germanicus)	
8		Death of Horace
c. 4		Birth of Seneca
CE		
14	Death of Augustus; Tiberius becomes emperor	
19		Death of Germanicus
20		Suicide of Piso

23		Death of Drusus the Younger; Tiberius retreats from Rome
31	Battle of Actium	
37	Death of Tiberius; Caligula becomes emperor	
41	Assassination of Caligula; Claudius becomes emperor	
54	Death of Claudius; Nero becomes emperor	
c. 56		Birth of Tacitus
c. 63		Publication of Seneca's *De Tranquillitate Animi*
c. 64		Publication of Seneca's *Epistulae Morales*
65		Suicide of Seneca
68	Suicide of Nero	
69	Year of the Four Emperors, concluding with Vespasian as emperor	
c. 69		Birth of Suetonius
79	Death of Vespasian; Titus becomes emperor	
81	Death of Titus; Domitian becomes emperor	
96	Assassination of Domitian; Nerva becomes emperor	
98	Death of Nerva; Trajan becomes emperor	
c. 117		Death of Tacitus

c. 117		Posthumous publication of Tacitus's *Annales*
117	Death of Trajan; Hadrian becomes emperor	
121		Publication of Suetonius's *De Vita Caesarum*
c. 122		Death of Suetonius

Appendix 2: Meter

— Dactylic Hexameter —

As its name describes, dactylic hexameter is comprised of six ("hex" is Greek for "six") dactyls ($-\ \smile\ \smile$). Two shorts can be replaced with one long, thereby making the foot a spondee ($-\ -$). The final foot is always a spondee because of the phenomenon known as *brevis in longo*: the final syllable in a line is considered long by position.

$$-\ \asymp\ |\ -\ \asymp\ |\ -\ \asymp\ |\ -\ \asymp\ |\ -\ \asymp\ |\ -\ -$$

For those who can read music, I often describe dactylic hexameter as six measures of 2/4 time: Each long syllable is a quarter note, and each short syllable is an eighth note. This analogy also reiterates that syllables are measured (and pronounced) by vowel length, rather than stress accent.

Dactylic hexameter is an unusually long meter, having between twelve and seventeen syllables per line. As a result, the content of the line is typically divided into at least two parts, delineated by punctuation, conjunctions, or a closural verb form (one that ends a phrase). This break in sense, called a *caesura* (from *caedo*, to cut) typically falls in the third or fourth foot (but not directly after the third foot).

— Alcaic Strophe —

The Alcaic strophe (or stanza) is Horace's favorite; it is named after the Greek lyric poet Alcaeus.

$$\times\ -\ \smile\ -\ \times\ |\ -\ \smile\ \smile\ -\ |\ \smile\ \times$$
$$\times\ -\ \smile\ -\ \times\ |\ -\ \smile\ \smile\ -\ |\ \smile\ \times$$
$$\times\ -\ \smile\ -\ |\ \times\ -\ \smile\ -\ |\ \times$$
$$-\ \smile\ \smile\ -\ \smile\ \smile\ -\ |\ \smile\ -\ -$$

— Sapphic Strophe —

The Sapphic strophe (or stanza) is also common in Horace; it is named after the Greek lyric poet Sappho.

$$- \cup - \times\ |\ - \cup \cup -\ |\ \cup - -$$
$$- \cup - \times\ |\ - \cup \cup -\ |\ \cup - -$$
$$- \cup - \times\ |\ - \cup \cup -\ |\ \cup - -$$
$$- \cup \cup -\ |\ -$$

— First Archilochian —

Named after the Greek lyric poet Archilochus, the first Archilochian is a couplet, of which the first line is dactylic hexameter and the second is a *hemiepes* (the first half of a line of dactylic hexameter). It is thus one and a half lines of dactylic hexameter:

$$- \underset{\smile\smile}{=}\ |\ - \underset{\smile\smile}{=}\ |\ - \underset{\smile\smile}{=}\ |\ - \underset{\smile\smile}{=}\ |\ - \underset{\smile\smile}{=}\ |\ - -$$
$$- \cup \cup\ |\ - \cup \cup\ |\ -$$

Appendix 3: Glossary of Rhetorical Terms, Figures of Speech, and Metrical Devices

alliteration: the use of the same consonant sound at the beginning of successive words.

anaphora: repetition of the same word at the beginning of successive clauses.

asyndeton: the omission of connecting conjunctions between clauses (compare **polysyndeton**).

chiasmus: words or clauses presented in ABBA form; that is, the second element reverses the order of the first.

diminutive: a noun that denotes a smaller version of another noun, often expressing affection.

ellipsis: when a word is omitted; very common with forms of *sum* in perfect passive verb forms.

enjambment: when the sense of a poetic line transgresses the line break and continues onto the next line.

euphemism: an expression of an unpleasant idea in more agreeable terms.

juxtaposition: the placement of two terms side by side in a striking manner.

litotes: expressing the positive by negating its opposite, e.g., "not unattractive."

metaphor: literally, a "carrying over" of a word to a new context: when a word or phrase is not meant literally, but figuratively.

personification: when an inanimate object is described in human terms.

polyptoton: the use of words from the same root, or forms of the same word, in close proximity.

polysyndeton: when an excess of conjunctions is used, frequently the excessive use of "and" or "or" in a list (compare **asyndeton**).

rhetorical question: a question to which the asker does not seek an actual answer.

simile: like **metaphor**, the figurative use of language to compare one object or situation to another.

synchysis: interlocking word order (ABAB form), as when an adjective is next to a noun with which it does not agree (compare **chiasmus**).

tricolon crescendo (*crescens*): a three-part construction, in which the first two elements are roughly half the length of the last.

variatio: variation in style of expression.

Appendix 4: Family Tree of the Julio-Claudians

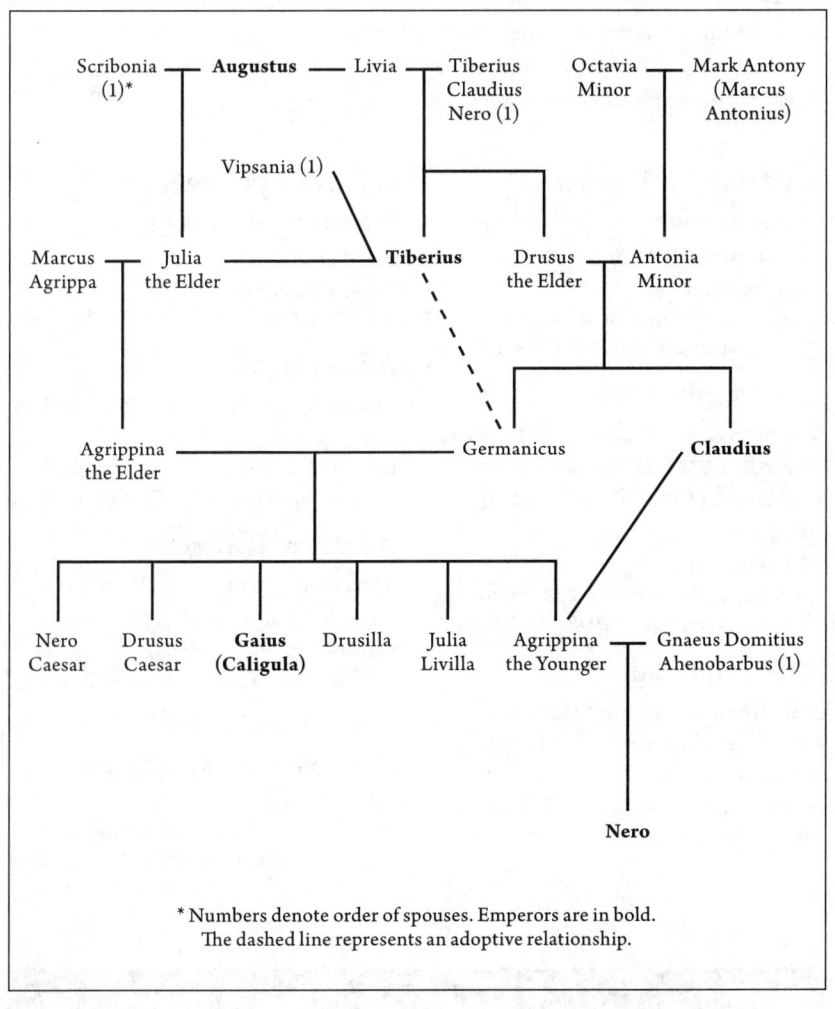

*Numbers denote order of spouses. Emperors are in bold.
The dashed line represents an adoptive relationship.

BC LATIN Readers

Series Editor: **Ronnie Ancona, Hunter College and CUNY Graduate Center**

These readers, written by experts in the field, provide well-annotated Latin selections to be used as authoritative introductions to Latin authors, genres, or topics. Designed for intermediate/advanced college Latin students, they each contain approximately 600 lines of Latin, making them ideal to use in combination or as a "shake-it-up" addition to a time-tested syllabus.

See reviews of BC Latin Readers from *Bryn Mawr Classical Review, Classical Outlook,* and more at http://www.bolchazy.com/readers/

An Apuleius Reader
Selections from the **Metamorphoses**
Ellen D. Finkelpearl
xxxviii + 160 pp., 4 illustrations & 1 map (2012)
5" x 7 ¾" Paperback, ISBN 978-0-86516-714-8

A Caesar Reader
Selections from **Bellum Gallicum** *and* **Bellum Civile,** *and from Caesar's Letters, Speeches, and Poetry*
W. Jeffrey Tatum
xl + 206 pp., 3 illustrations & 3 maps (2012)
5" x 7 ¾" Paperback, ISBN 978-0-86516-696-7

A Cicero Reader
Selections from Five Essays and Four Speeches, with Five Letters
James M. May
xxxviii + 136 pp., 1 illustration & 2 maps (2012)
5" x 7 ¾" Paperback, ISBN 978-0-86516-713-1

A Latin Epic Reader
Selections from Ten Epics
Alison Keith
xxvii + 187 pp., 3 maps (2012)
5" x 7 ¾" Paperback, ISBN 978-0-86516-686-8

A Livy Reader
Selections from **Ab Urbe Condita**
Mary Jaeger
xxiii + 127 pp., 1 photo & 2 maps (2010)
5" x 7 ¾" Paperback, ISBN 978-0-86516-680-6

A Lucan Reader
Selections from **Civil War**
Susanna Braund
xxxiv + 134 pp., 1 map (2009)
5" x 7 ¾" Paperback, ISBN 978-0-86516-661-5

A Martial Reader
Selections from the Epigrams
Craig Williams
xxx + 185 pp., 5 illustrations & 2 maps (2011)
5" x 7 ¾" Paperback, ISBN 978-0-86516-704-9

Bolchazy-Carducci Publishers, Inc.
www.BOLCHAZY.com

An Ovid Reader
Selections from Seven Works
Carole E. Newlands
xxvi + 196 pp., 5 illustrations (2014)
5" x 7 ¾" Paperback, ISBN 978-0-86516-722-3

A Plautus Reader
Selections from Eleven Plays
John Henderson
xviii + 182 pp., 1 map & 5 illustrations (2009)
5" x 7 ¾" Paperback, ISBN 978-0-86516-694-3

A Propertius Reader
Eleven Selected Elegies
P. Lowell Bowditch
xliv + 186 pp., 5 illustrations & 2 maps (2014)
5" x 7 ¾" Paperback, ISBN 978-0-86516-723-0

A Roman Army Reader
Twenty-One Selections from Literary, Epigraphic, and Other Documents
Dexter Hoyos
xlviii + 214 pp., 7 illustrations & 2 maps (2013)
5" x 7 ¾" Paperback, ISBN 978-0-86516-715-5

A Roman Verse Satire Reader
Selections from Lucilius, Horace, Persius, and Juvenal
Catherine C. Keane
xxvi + 142 pp., 1 map & 4 illustrations (2010)
5" x 7 ¾" Paperback, ISBN 978-0-86516-685-1

A Roman Women Reader
Selections from the Second Century BCE to the Second Century CE
Sheila K. Dickison and Judith P. Hallett
xxii + 225 pp., 3 illustrations (2015)
5" x 7 ¾" Paperback, ISBN 978-0-86516-662-2

A Sallust Reader
Selections from BELLUM CATILINAE, BELLUM IUGURTHINUM, and HISTORIAE
Victoria E. Pagán
xlv + 159 pp., 2 maps & 4 illustrations (2009)
5" x 7 ¾" Paperback, ISBN 978-0-86516-687-5

A Seneca Reader
Selections from Prose and Tragedy
James Ker
lvi + 166 pp., 6 illustrations & 1 map (2011)
5" x 7 ¾" Paperback, ISBN 978-0-86516-758-2

A Suetonius Reader
Selections from the LIVES OF THE CAESARS and the LIFE OF HORACE
Josiah Osgood
xxxix + 159 pp., 1 map & 7 illustrations (2010)
5" x 7 ¾" Paperback, ISBN 978-0-86516-716-2

A Tacitus Reader
Selections from ANNALES, HISTORIAE, GERMANIA, AGRICOLA, and DIALOGUS
Steven H. Rutledge
xlvii + 198 pp., 5 illustrations, 2 maps, & 3 charts (2014) 5" x 7 ¾" Paperback
ISBN 978-0-86516-697-4

A Terence Reader
Selections from Six Plays
William S. Anderson
xvii + 110 pp. (2009) 5" x 7 ¾" Paperback, ISBN 978-0-86516-678-3

A Tibullus Reader
Seven Selected Elegies
Paul Allen Miller
xx + 132 pp., 2 illustrations (2013) 5" x 7 ¾" Paperback, ISBN 978-0-86516-724-7

BOLCHAZY-CARDUCCI PUBLISHERS, INC.
WWW.BOLCHAZY.COM

Annotated Latin Collection

Read Catullus, Cicero, Horace, and Ovid with these well-annotated texts designed for intermediate to advanced students. With same-page notes and vocabulary, introductory essays on each author and work, full glossaries, and helpful appendices, reading unadapted Latin has never been more rewarding.

Cicero: Pro Archia Poeta Oratio 3rd Edition
Steven M. Cerutti

xxxi + 157 pp. (2014) 6" x 9" Paperback, ISBN 9780-86516-805-3

This text contains the entire oration (**397 lines**). This revised edition includes input from Linda A. Fabrizio, author of the Teacher's Guide, and a new appendix featuring eight selections from Quintilian.

Horace: Selected Odes and Satire 1.9
Ronnie Ancona

xxxiii + 171 pp., 4 maps (2014, 2nd edition revised) 6" x 9" Paperback, ISBN 978-0-86516-608-0

Contains (**533 lines**) *Odes* 1.1, 5, 9, 11, 13, 22, 23, 24, 25, 37, 38; 2.3, 7, 10, 14; 3.1, 9, 13, 30; *Satire* 1.9. The revised second edition features an updated bibliography and more visually appealing maps.

Ovid: Amores, Metamorphoses Selections, 3rd Edition
Phyllis B. Katz and Charbra Adams Jestin

xxx + 212 pp. (2013) 6" x 9" Paperback, ISBN 978-0-86516-784-1

Amores I.1, I.3, I.9, I.11, I.12, III.12, III.15; *Metamorphoses* I.1–88 (Creation), I.452–567 (Apollo and Daphne), IV.55–166 (Pyramus and Thisbe), VIII.183–235 (Daedalus and Icarus), VIII.616–723 (Philemon and Baucis), X.1–85 (Orpheus), and X.238–297 (Pygmalion). **907 lines**.

Bolchazy-Carducci Publishers, Inc.
www.bolchazy.com

Writing Passion: *A Catullus Reader* 2nd Edition
Ronnie Ancona

xl + 264 pp. (2013) 6" x 9" Paperback, ISBN 978-0-86516-786-5

Four additional poems expand the elegiac selections about Lesbia. This text includes (**827** lines) Catullus 1–5, 7–8, 10–14a, 22, 30–31, 35–36, 40, 43–46, 49–51, 60, 64 (lines 50–253), 65, 68 (lines 1–40), 69–70, 72, 75–77, 83–87, 92, 96, 101, 107, 109, 116.

Writing Passion Plus
A Catullus Reader Supplement
Ronnie Ancona

ix + 22 pp. (2013) 6" x 9" Paperback, ISBN 978-0-86516-788-9

For those who want a little more spice in their Catullus, this text provides poems 6, 16, 32, and 57 (**52 lines**).

Watch for New Editions of These Popular Texts

Cicero: *Pro Caelio*, 3rd Edition
Stephen Ciraolo

xxxi + 239 pp. (2010) 6" x 9" Paperback, ISBN 978-0-86516-559-5

This user-friendly text features the entire oration (**991 lines**) with vocabulary and commentary on grammar, style, history, and Roman institutions; introductory essays on the lives of Cicero and Caelius and on Roman oratory; and several appendices.

Cicero: *De Amicitia Selections*
Patsy Rodden Ricks and Sheila K. Dickison

x + 73 pp. (2006) 6" x 9" Paperback, ISBN 978-0-86516-639-4

This text, which contains *De Amicitia* V.17–VII.23 (**199 lines**), makes for a great introduction to Cicero. Vocabulary, notes, English overviews of the missing sections of the *De Amicitia*, and a Glossary of Figures of Speech complete this text.

LATIN POETRY

Catullus: *Expanded Edition*
Phyllis Young Forsyth and Henry V. Bender

xii + 140 pp. (2005) 8½" x 11" Paperback, ISBN 978-0-86516-603-5

This student-friendly text offers (**805 lines**) Catullus 1–5, 7, 8, 10–14a, 22, 30, 31, 35, 36, 40, 43–46, 49–51, 60, 64 (lines 50–253), 65, 68–70, 72, 76, 77, 84–87, 96, 101, 109, and 116.

Lucretius: *Selections from DE RERUM NATURA*
Bonnie A. Catto

xxx + 272 pp. (1998) 8½" x 11 Paperback, ISBN 978-0-86516-399-7

This text provides 53 passages (**1,291 lines**) spanning the entire epic. Each section features a short introduction, discussion questions, vocabulary and line-by-line notes on facing pages, and a variety of illustrative quotations from ancient and modern authors.

The *Thebaid* of Statius: *The Women of Lemnos*
Patrick Yaggy

xxvii + 242 pp. (2014) 6" x 9" Paperback, ISBN 978-0-86516-819-0

The high-interest story of Hypsipyle and the women of Lemnos (*Thebaid* 5.1–637) makes the perfect introduction to Statius's *Thebaid* for intermediate readers of Latin (**637 lines**).

Vergil's *Aeneid: Expanded Collection*
Barbara Weiden Boyd

xl + 449 pp. (2013) 6" x 9" Paperback, ISBN 978-0-86516-789-6

This well-annotated Latin text (**2,596 lines**) makes the perfect introduction to Vergil's *Aeneid*. Passages include 1.1–756 • 2.1–56; 199–297; 469–620; 735–805 • 4.1–449; 642–705 • 6.1–211; 295–332; 384–425; 450–476; 847–901 • 8.608–731 • 10.420–509 • 11.498–596; 664–835 • 12.791–842; 887–952.

BOLCHAZY-CARDUCCI PUBLISHERS, INC.
WWW.BOLCHAZY.COM

Latin Prose

Caesar: *Selections from his* COMMENTARII DE BELLO GALLICO
Hans-Friedrich Mueller

xlii + 372 pp. (2012) 6" x 9"
Paperback, ISBN 978-0-86516-752-0 • Hardbound, ISBN 978-0-86516-778-0

This text provides (**827 lines**) *De Bello Gallico* 1.1–7; 4.24–35 and the first sentence of chapter 36; 5.24–48; 6.13–20 with same-page vocabulary and notes. Annotated English passages from Books 1, 6, and 7 provide additional context for the Latin passages.

Cicero's First Catilinarian Oration
Karl Frerichs

xviii + 62 pp. (1997, reprint 2000, 2004) 8½" x 11 Paperback
ISBN 978-0-86516-341-6

This edition provides the entire speech (**317 lines**) with the essential vocabulary and assistance students need. A historical narrative introduces the oration

Res Gestae Divi Augusti
Rex E. Wallace

xxii + 80 pp. (2000, on demand 2007) 6" x 9" Paperback
ISBN 978-0-86516-455-0

The *Res Gestae* (**327 lines**) reveals as much about Augustus through what it omits as what it contains. This edition allows students rare access to nonliterary historical Latin.

Seneca's Moral Epistles
Anna Lydia Motto

xxxi + 213 pp. (2001, on demand 2007) 6" x 9" Paperback
ISBN 978-0-86516-487-1

An intriguing selection of 40 letters (**2,724 lines**) of Seneca in Latin on philosophical and practical topics provides a fascinating glimpse into daily life in Rome. Selections are Epistles 1–3, 5–7, 11, 12, 15, 16, 18, 21, 23, 27, 28, 34, 37, 38, 41–44, 47, 50, 52–54, 56, 60–63, 72, 80, 84, 90, 96, 112, 114.

Bolchazy-Carducci Publishers, Inc.
www.BOLCHAZY.com

Lectiones Memorabiles
Volume I
Selections from Catullus, Cicero, Livy, Ovid, Propertius, Tibullus, and Vergil

Marianthe Colakis

xii + 341 pp. (2015) 6" x 9" Paperback
ISBN 978-0-86516-829-9

This student-friendly annotated Latin text offers selections from Latin prose and poetry. Same- and facing-page notes aid students in understanding the text and context of a diverse body of Latin literature. Introductions to each author and to each selection offer additional support.

Features

- Unadapted Latin text
- Introduction to each author and to each poem or selection
- Latin text with same- and facing-page notes
- Appendices on meter and on literary terms
- Historical and literary timelines

This volume provides prescribed passages for the IB Latin Syllabus with examinations in 2016, 2017, and 2018. *Lectiones Memorabiles: Volume I: Selections from Catullus, Cicero, Livy, Ovid, Propertius, Tibullus, and Vergil* contains all Standard Level and Higher Level readings required for **Vergil**, **Love Poetry**, and **Women**.

Selections include Vergil, *Aeneid* 1.1–49, 223–493; 11.648–724; *Georgics* 4.315–529 • Catullus, *Carmina* 3, 5, 7, 8, 9, 45, 50, 64.48–158, 65, 72, 76, 85, 86, 92, 107, 109 • Propertius, *Elegies* 1.1, 2.12, 2.17, 2.19, 3.11, 3.23 • Tibullus, *Elegies* 1.1, 3.2, 3.3, 3.13, 3.14, 3.15, 3.16, 3.17, 3.18 • Ovid, *Heroides* 1 • Livy, *Ab Urbe Condita* 2.13 • Cicero, *Pro Caelio* 35–40 • Horace, *Carmina* 1.37.

This work has been developed independently from
and is not endorsed by the International Baccalaureate (IB).

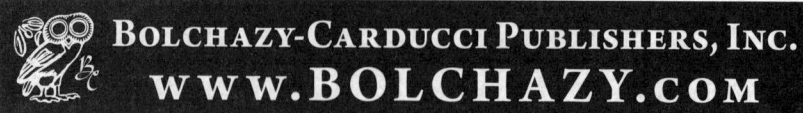